FINAL TRUTH

The Autobiography of
Pee Wee Gaskins

MONSTER PUBLISHING
monsterpublishing77@gmail.com

Copyright © 2021 Monster Publishing.

All rights reserved, including the right to reproduce this book or portions thereof in any form whatsoever.

The following words were spoken by Pee Wee Gaskins
in the months leading up to his death in the
South Carolina electric chair on September 6, 1991.

1

I did most of what I call my serious murders, the ones where I actually knowed the people that I killed, in Florence and Sumter Counties, South Carolina, the same part of the state where I grew up. It's mainly farms and woods, backwaters, and swamps, and little towns with names like Lake City and Johnsonville, and other spots not hardly big enough to be put on a map: Prospect, and Leo, and Roper's Crossroads, and The Neck. It was a good place to lead my kind of life. There was lots of places to bury bodies.

Being born on a farm, I know the difference between raising something and it just growing. You raise tobacco and vegetables to harvest, and pigs and sheep to butcher. They got purpose, you tend them. But weeds grow on their own, tended or not. I grew. I weren't raised. That's for damn sure. Hell, I didn't know my own real name until I was a teenager and got sentenced to the reformatory. Up until then, at home and at school, my name had always been Junior Parrott and everybody everywhere called me Junior or Pee Wee Parrott, which made sense to me because my Mama's name was Parrott and far as I knew, my whole family was named Parrott except for my stepdaddies. None of them was named Parrott, but then nobody ever has the same name as their stepdaddy.

When the judge sentenced me to the reformatory until age eighteen, he said I was lucky I was a juvenile, otherwise he would have put me away for a really long time for what I'd done. Then he looked at my arrest report and asked why I had my Mama's name? Where was my daddy? What was *his* name?

And Mama didn't lie to him like she did to everybody else. She said I had her name because she never had married my daddy and that my true name as it was writ in the family Bible, was Donald Henry Gaskins, Jr. For a minute I thought the judge was going to shit right there on the bench. "You sure about that?" he said. And my Mama said she was real sure. She was fifteen when I was born and Donald Henry Gaskins was the only man who had ever done it to her before she got pregnant with me. And he had even helped her with support money until she married my stepdaddy. She told me later that the real reason my real daddy had give her money was to keep her quiet about him being my father, but she still believed he would have married her if he hadn't been so well off that his family wouldn't let him.

When I was younger, there was always one or another of a bunch of different stepdaddies around. I called them all sir and never bothered to learn most of their names because I knew my Mama wasn't married to them and they wouldn't likely be around for long. The one she finally did marry was one mean son of a bitch. He used to back hand me and knock me clean across the room just for practice. But then everybody knocked me around, my uncles, my other stepdaddies, and nearabout all the boys and girls I played with and went to school with. They beat up on me just because I was so damned little.

It weren't that I was the littlest because I was youngest, no matter how old I got, I was still littlest. I never growed enough to keep up with the others. That's how I got the nickname Pee Wee. "Pee Wee, Pee Wee playing with your Pee Pee," they used to say. And when I'd get mad and hit somebody, that was all the excuse they needed to gang up and beat hell out of me.

I was born March 31, 1933, and most of what I remember from when I was real young is hazy, like trying to see through smoke in the woods, but I do have this here one memory from before I started school that's as clear as yesterday. Going to the carnival.

Most of my stepdaddies was tight as a preacher's asshole when it come to money except for one. The year he lived with my Mama I reckon he had made a good share. It was about 1937 I would guess and a little carnival had set up along the state highway between Lake City and Johnsonville and my then stepdaddy decided we was going to see it.

I remember him, and Mama, and me, and a girl cousin who was almost little as me walking along a sawdust midway and stopping in front of a tent with paintings on it of a snake wrapped around a big titted woman and an alligator swallowing a whole cow. My stepdaddy paid a dime apiece for him and Mama and a nickel each for me and my cousin. Inside the tent, in a wire pen was this alligator that didn't look very big to me, even then, and inside of glass front cages there was bunches of snakes all balled up, sleeping, I guessed.

The man who took our money outside followed us in and talked to us through a megaphone which he didn't hardly need because there weren't nobody else there but us. He was a barker I learned later when I worked carnivals. And I remember him saying something like, "ladies and gentlemen let me direct your attention to the center of the tent. The snake lying inside that cage may look peaceful, but don't be fooled, you are looking at the most dangerous creature on God's earth. That is the fearsome King Cobra that each year kills hundreds, some years thousands, of men, women, and children in India."

Then the barker stopped talking, took a live rat out of a box and dropped it in the cage with the snake. That rat ran around and around real fast. The Cobra stirred and coiled, rose up, and flared out its neck. And the rat stopped and froze like it thought that if it stayed still, it might turn invisible.

What took hold of my attention right then was that that Cobra's head was almost exactly as high up as my head. When I looked through the glass, I was staring it straight in the eye, and my reflection looked like that Cobra and me had the same head and face and eyes.

Then the barker said, "a Cobra eats twice a week. This one was fed last night. That bulge halfway down its length is the supper it is still digesting. So let me assure you, this snake is not hungry. And as you no doubt noticed when you walked up to its cage the Cobra didn't get upset. It just lay there. That's because it is used to people and knew it didn't need to defend itself. But now suddenly it has raised itself up and is about ready to strike. And that, ladies and gentlemen, is what makes the Cobra the most dangerous of all reptiles! The fact that even as we watch it it is preparing to kill for no reason other than the fact that it has decided to kill."

The snake struck, then stretched out and went back to sleep. The rat didn't move. I looked at my reflection, then at the Cobra and I turned and saw my girl cousin holding tight to my Mama's leg, and I looked up at my Mama's and stepdaddy's faces and saw that they seemed pretty scared, too. I had a hard on. And I knew that what I had just seen was somehow special and important, even though I didn't know why. I still carry that memory, clear as a picture etched on my brain. Nothing they do to me can ever burn it away.

But I can't say there was much else about them years spent growing up on a tobacco farm outside of Leo, South Carolina that was worth remembering.

To me, school was more than just a waste, it was a kind of torture. Everybody picked on me, so I got into fights almost everyday and then I got punished by the teachers and principal for fighting. It's no wonder I never learned jack shit.

About the onliest thing that truly interested me when I was a boy, and still does, was figuring out what made things work, especially cars and things electric, like radios. I was a pretty good tinkerer by the time I was ten. "That Pee Wee can fix anything," Mama use to say.

Before I was ten, I was hanging around the mechanic at the filling station a few miles down the highway and when I was eleven I was laying out of school about half the time making a dollar or two a day helping tote and fetch and do. When I up and quit school, my Mama was real unhappy. My stepdaddy said that if I weren't going to school I had to work in the fields and do more chores. I said I wanted to work on cars, not on a farm, but he beat my ass so bad every time I slipped off to work for the mechanic that I decided it was best just to do what he wanted. Then after a while, thanks to my Mama, he agreed that on Saturdays I could go work at the station.

Not far from where we lived there was this old house that had been empty for years. Most Sunday afternoons, and any other time I could, I went there to meet up with other boys from around Leo. We called it our hide out. We sat around and smoked cigarettes we had stole and bragged about how much we knew about girls, and we watched the older boys and learned how to jerk off or cornhole or fuck a sheep or goat or chicken. And we usually ended up fighting about something.

I remember that the worst whipping I ever got was the time me and two older boys dug a trench back of the outhouse at the church so we could hide there and watch the women and girls when they pulled down their pants. Three sets of stepdaddies, a preacher, a deacon, and four mamas, including my Mama, joined together and tore our asses to ribbons with switches for that.

Even back then girls pissed me off. The way I saw it, they had something boys wanted, but wouldn't even let a boy look at it, much less fuck it, unless the boy did whatever the girl wanted. It specially made me mad that them bitches could do anything they wanted, show their asses, make fun of me, even beat me up and dare me to do anything about it, knowing I couldn't do nothing without being punished by grownups.

But don't get me wrong, my childhood weren't all that bad all the time. I certainly weren't in no way what you could ever call abused. final truth is, for the most part, my family life was pretty good. I had two sisters and two brothers. I reckon half-sisters and half-brothers is more correct. They was all a lot younger than me cause they wasn't borned until after I started school and my Mama finally married my legal stepdaddy, Hinnant Hanna, who was truly mean as hell and is dead now. So is one of my half-brothers.

My Mama was a real good cook and we always had enough to eat. Most days, after I had quit going to school, I did my chores, and minded my manners, and stayed out of trouble, and my brothers and sisters did their chores and didn't mess with me. They was even nice to me sometimes, usually when something of theirs was broke and they wanted me to fix it.

I had a good little business going. On Saturdays, people brought broken radios and record players and sewing machines and things like that to the gas station and I took them home and repaired them in the evenings. I worked in a corner of the parlor room, which was also where me and my brothers slept. The whole family sat in there after supper because that was where the radio was and we listened to The Shadow and The Lone Ranger and The Grand Old Opry and all kinds of good programs like that.

Mama was most always sewing, while my stepdaddy smoked his pipe, and sipped corn, and talked back to the radio, and my sisters and brothers played and teased. I remember my house and my family usually being like that. Good and peaceful. But no matter how things went, good or bad, I always felt something bothersome was astirring inside me. It was like I had this ball of plumber's lead rolling around in my guts. Most times it lay quiet, just weighting me down. Other times, it growed bigger and hotter, like it was going to explode. Every once in a while I dreamed, I still do, that it blowed me apart and there was all these millions of little pieces and parts of me running around and flying around trying to find each other and put me back together.

2

My Mama got upset about every little scrape I got into after I quit school. My stepdaddy shrugged most of it off and said, "boys will be boys," then knocked shit out of me and told me to straighten up and quit causing my Mama worry.

What I was doing didn't amount to much. I teamed up with two boys who become my onliest and best friends during them years. I had got to know them at The Hideout. Their names was Danny and Marsh. We broke open vending machines and stole money and cigarettes and drinks and hid most of what we stole in the loft of my Mama's barn until one of my sisters found everything and told on me. My stepdaddy wanted to know who was doing the stealing with me. I swore I was doing it all by myself. He threatened to take me to the sheriff if I ever did it again.

After that, me and Danny and Marsh named our selfs The Trouble Trio. They was older than me, but I was the leader because I hadn't ratted them out and because I was the one who had come up with this here really good idea for us to make money. Like I already said, I had a good little business repairing radios, and victrolas, and sewing machines, and other things like that, that people brought to me to fix and one Saturday a man that lived seven or eight miles away come to the gas station and said he had a floor model radio that was broke but was too big to bring in so I went to his house with him and fixed it there. And that's when my idea came to me.

His house was full of all kinds of things that was worth money and I knew I could figure a way to break in and steal them if only I could find a place to sell them. This was while World War Two was going on and gas was rationed. In South Carolina you could get a driver's license when you was fourteen. I wasn't old enough to have one, but Danny did, and what's more his daddy had a pickup truck that he let us ride around in provided we always brought it back with a full tank of gas. Danny's daddy had done time in Georgia for burglary, armed robbery, and assault, and he was tough as cement, but he wasn't never mean to Danny or Marsh or me. I really did like him.

And, of course, he knew we didn't have no gas ration coupons and that we was stealing gas at night from highway stations twenty or thirty miles away. They had those glass top hand pumps. A crowbar and a ball-peen hammer was all it took to knock open the padlocks on them so it was easy for us to get the gas we needed for our riding around and to keep Danny's daddy's truck filled up, too.

When I told Danny and Marsh my idea about breaking in houses, Danny went straight to his daddy for advice and his daddy offered to fence for us. That was the first time I ever heard that word used that way. He knew men in Augusta who would pay top dollar for certain things. He told us the best time to break in country homes, Saturday afternoons, and how to check out houses to make sure nobody was home. Then he told us what things to steal, which ones would bring the most money, and the kinds of things that fences wouldn't touch because they could be traced. Then we started breaking and entering, and the three of us in The Trouble Trio was in business for almost two years.

We followed Danny's daddy's advice about everything. He never cheated us. We trusted him so much we let him keep our money in his house and, when we had enough saved up, he used it to buy a '36 Ford for us. We had money, but we didn't flash it because Danny's daddy said that wouldn't be smart. It was best if folks thought he owned the Ford and just let us use it.

Sometimes we headed to Columbia or Charleston where there was military bases and plenty of whores. That's how we all three lost our pussy fuck cherries. But there was something about them whores that we didn't like. We agreed that jacking off at The Hideout was almost as good.

Marsh thought The Hideout was better than whores. He liked cornholing the younger boys and letting them corn hole him. And he liked to suck dicks. Danny and me didn't go for that too much. Mostly we just watched, though to be honest, like most teenage boys, we tried it all once or more, and because Marsh was our friend, we would let him suck us off whenever he asked to.

Most girls our age wouldn't go out with us because we had all three quit school and were considered wild and let it be known that the back seat of our Ford was for fucking. There were some who were agreeable, mostly ones Danny knew, but even though they didn't charge money for their pussy, they had fucked so many boys they weren't any tighter and tenderer than them old worn out military whores.

One evening when we was just riding around, smoking and talking, Marsh said that what we needed was a virgin, or at least a tender young piece. That was the only way we was ever going to find out what young pussy felt and smelled and tasted like. Me and Danny agreed, and that was when we hatched the idea to find a girl and take her to The Hideout and rape her. Of course, we knew our plan could spell real trouble, we had to be careful who we picked. Marsh suggested his youngest sister. She was thirteen and he said that after we done it, it would be easy to convince her not to tell anybody. We agreed she was a good choice.

I told the mechanic I couldn't work but a half day that next Saturday. Marsh's mama said it was okay for his little sister to go with him and us to a double feature afternoon movie in Sumter. Like me, Marsh didn't have a daddy, just a bunch of different stepdaddies. The main difference was his mama was boss at his house, no stepdaddy had any say about anything. His mama was a real big lady, but I'm getting ahead of my story. Anyhow, we took Marsh's sister to The Hideout, not to the movie, and we held her down, and took off her clothes, and smelled, and tasted her cracks, and sucked her tiny little titties, and made her suck our dicks. Then we fucked her and corn holed her.

We each come I don't know how many times. It was like we couldn't get enough. But even though we didn't hit her or do nothing to hurt her, she still cried and begged us to stop. But we just couldn't, it was too good. When we finally finished with her and it came time to take her home, we promised to give her all kinds of money if she didn't tell anybody what we'd done. Then we told her that if she did tell anybody, we would hurt her real bad. We said everything we could think up to make sure she wouldn't tell nobody.

finally, she stopped crying and promised she wouldn't say a word. Danny and I gave her our under shirts to wipe herself with and Marsh went to the well and brought water so she could clean herself up. By the time she was washed and dressed, she looked just about the same as she had when we started out to the movie earlier. We went to a drive-in and got burgers, but she didn't eat much, though she did drink her Orange Crush.

Danny and me took her and Marsh to their house about supper time. Her folks weren't home yet from their Saturday shopping. We left them then Danny took me to my house, and he drove on home. The weather was real warm, so, after supper, my family and me went out and sat on the front porch and listened to the parlor radio that was turned on loud to the Opry. Marsh's mama was driving the car that come barreling into our front yard, skidded right up to the porch steps and stopped.

She bounced out and grabbed me and before I could say or do shit she knocked me aside the head with her fist and I dropped like a rock, out cold. That lady was big, mean and strong.

When I come to, I was still lying on the ground and my family had all gone in the house except for my stepdaddy. He was standing a few feet away from me, next to Marsh's stepdaddy and Marsh. Marsh's mama was standing practically on top of me. She called me every unchristian kind of name she could think of and punctuated every one with a kick to my gut. And she was wearing brogans. I rolled and moaned. Next thing I knew, they was dragging Marsh and me to the barn. They stripped Marsh first, roped his ankles together, and threw the rope over a joist, and strung him upside down. Then his mama commenced to paddle him with a pine slat. Soon his ass was bleeding and then she told his stepdaddy to whup him with his belt. After just a little while Marsh's back and legs was a bloody mess. He didn't move when they let him down.

Then it was my turn to be strung up naked. I felt the pine board splitting my butt, then my stepdaddy stropped me with his belt like I hadn't never been stropped before. The pain was all in my back and legs, my ass had already went numb. I was just about to pass out when I heard Marsh's mama scream, "you god damn little piece of shit I ought to cut it off right here and now!" I realized I had a hard on.

She didn't cut it off, but she did take the belt from my stepdaddy and she stropped my dick and balls until I thought sure they would be useless to me for the rest of my life. When they finally lowered me down to the barn floor and left me, I couldn't move. I stayed there all night, turning colder ever minute, hurting too bad to get up and put my clothes on, afraid to try to crawl to the house.

I know Marsh's mama told my Mama what we had done, but I don't think Mama ever told my sisters and brothers. Leastwise they never mentioned it to me. Fact is, neither did my Mama or my stepdaddy. The whole incident wasn't never talked about except once when my stepdaddy said that if I ever did anything like that again, he was going to take me to the sheriff.

Marsh's mama didn't want folks to know what happened because it would ruin his little sister's reputation, that's what Marsh told me the next morning when I went to The Hideout while my folks was in church. I still hurt so much I could hardly walk, but I figured Danny and Marsh would get there if they could and I needed to see them.

Other than the big knot on the side of my head, all my bruises and cuts was covered by clothes. But Marsh's mama had done a prize fighter job on his face. He looked like he had gone ten rounds with Joe Louis. He said he was afraid that if he stayed around home, his mama was just going to get madder and madder at him and beat him more and more, and sooner or later probably kill him, so he was going to run away from home. He had a suitcase of stuff with him ready to go.

Danny arrived a few minutes after I did. He was driving the Ford and didn't have a mark on him. He said that as soon as he got home, he had told his daddy that we fucked Marsh's sister and that he was worried that because she was young she might tell her mama it was rape.

Danny's daddy had stayed real calm and told him to go to the kitchen and wait there. When Marsh's mama and stepdaddy got to Danny's house, a few minutes after they left my house, Danny's daddy was sitting on the front porch with a shotgun across his lap and a revolver in his belt and told them that if any of them so much as stepped out of the car he would blow a hole in them. Then he told them they weren't even going to see Danny, much less punish him, that it weren't like we had really hurt Marsh's sister. Sure, her pussy had bled a little bit, but it would be good as new in a few days, so why was they so upset? And then he warned them that if they went to the law and had Danny arrested, he would kill their whole fucking family.

Marsh's mama and stepdaddy took Danny's daddy at his word and just drove away with Marsh moaning on the back seat. Danny's daddy told Danny that he thought it might be a good idea if him and Danny went to Texas for a few weeks, or maybe months. Pained as we was, me and Marsh couldn't help smiling. How great it must be to have a daddy like Danny's daddy. Danny could always count on him to take his side.

Marsh said again that he wasn't going to wait around, he was going to run away that very day. Danny said he understood, and we would take him to

Sumter to catch a bus, but first we should go get Marsh's share of the money that Danny's daddy was holding for him. We piled in the Ford and went to Danny's house. His daddy couldn't have been nicer. He gave Marsh his share of the money then gave me my share. Then we drove Marsh to the bus station in Sumpter.

Marsh gave me a hug, which made me and him both flinch, we was so bruised. Then he hugged Danny and managed a smile, even though I think he was crying, and he said he would write to us care of the general delivery at Johnsonville. We waited around until his bus left and he waved goodbye. I got postcards from him, time to time, and a letter once, but I never saw him again.

Danny drove me home and said how bad and sad he felt seeing The Trouble Trio separating. I agreed. We shook hands, then we hugged, and promised we would write, and we would see each other soon as we could. Two days later, when I went by his house, Danny and his daddy had done gone. The next month I got an envelope at the Johnsonville post office. It was postmarked Atlanta and in it was seventy-five dollars and a note from Danny saying that was my share of the sale of the Ford.

Probably the best part of my life had just ended. Only I didn't know it. I tried to go back to how it was, but nothing seemed to want to go back with me. The bothersome weight got heavier and hotter. At the gas station a few months later I heard that Marsh's mama had sold her house, and twenty acres, and moved to Arkansas. I kept my repair business going, but I weren't happy. I had got used to going to see a movie whenever I wanted to, or shopping with a few dollars in my pocket, or even going as far as Charleston and Columbia whore hopping, but now I either stayed home or went to the gas station or The Hideout. At least now the boys there showed me some respect because they had heard all the stories about The Trouble Trio.

Sometime later at the gas station I met a man who'd been stationed at the naval base in North Charleston during the war and had married a Columbia girl. They were driving to Charleston in his brand new Chevy coupe when it blew a water hose not three miles from the gas station where I was working. Him and me got to talking while I was putting on the new hose. I was real impressed by his Navy stories which, from the bored expression on his wife's face, she had heard plenty of times before.

When I finished with the hose, I walked around back to wash up. It was one more hot day. He came around and took a piss on the side of the building and asked me if there was any way to make any money around here without working too hard. I said that depended on what he was willing to do. He said he had done juvenile time for breaking and entering and considered reform school a good education.

I told him there might be some things worth stealing in a few houses out in the country if we had a place to sell what was stole. Walt said he could handle the fencing and would pay me for certain things that he knew he could resell in Charleston. Then he proceeded to tell me what was worth stealing and I interrupted and finished the list for him and right then and there we had an understanding.

After that, Walt picked me up near The Hideout every other Saturday afternoon and we drove to a house I had chose. He waited while I broke in and stole. Then we went back to The Hideout and he paid me for the things I had put in his trunk. He paid low dollar, but I was saving up to buy me a car so I needed the money and took whatever he gave.

Then, on the last Saturday of the third month we did business, everything turned to shit. I had chose a house not too far from my Mama's because I knew the family that lived there had gone to a funeral up in Lexington County. That's a good time to hit rural houses, during church services, or weddings, or funerals.

Walt parked in the edge of the woods not far from the house so he could see if anyone came and blow the horn to warn me. I went to the door to force it open, and it was unlocked. I remember smiling to myself and thinking how easy this one was going to be. I walked through the kitchen and god damned if there wasn't a girl in there I knowed standing there with a hatchet in her hand!

She said, "Junior, what are you doing in here?" Then she swung at me. I run out the door and damned if she didn't come after me. I was looking back to see if she was gaining on me and I stumbled on a tree root, and fell down, and she caught up to me and swung at me again. I grabbed her arm, wrenched the hatchet away from her, and hit her twice on her arms which she raised up to try to protect herself. Then I used the blunt side to knock her in the head. She dropped to the ground. I hit her a couple of more times on the back. She didn't move.

Then I heard somebody coming out the back door and I ran like crazy and had barely got into the edge of the woods when I heard the shotgun blast and buckshot sprinkled the trees around me. When I come out of the other side of the woods, Walt's car was already half a mile down the road and it suddenly occurred to me that I didn't know nothing about him, not even his last name, much less where he lived. The only thing I knowed for sure was that he was one chicken shit son of a bitch.

I headed cross-country to my Mama's house. The sheriff and two deputies got there ten minutes after I did. They took me to jail, printed and pictured me, then locked me in the holding room where they kept juveniles. The lawmen told me that the girl I had hit with the hatchet was in the hospital in terrible bad condition. Her aunt, who had heard her scream and grabbed the shotgun and shot at me from the back door, come straight down to the jail and identified me.

The charge put against me was assault with a deadly weapon with intent to kill. For my charge, they sentenced me to the South Carolina Industrial School For Boys, better knowed as the state reformatory.

My real education was about to begin.

3

They didn't send me far. The South Carolina Reform School For Boys was located on National Cemetery Road, east of the town of Florence, only a few miles from Leo where I growed up. With its dormitories and school buildings separated by hedges, gardens and pastures it looked more like a college campus than a prison.

There weren't no towers or guns and not many guards. The supervisors assigned us to classes like carpentry, and mechanics, and metal working to teach us a trade and, after classes, they put us on work details in the fields and barns. We got demerits if we sassed the overseers or broke the rules, which weren't all that unreasonable. I probably would've got along all right there if the things that went on at night had been different.

Between suppertime and reveille the dormitory doors were locked from the outside and, unless a fire alarm sounded, they weren't opened for any reason. Once we was locked inside we had to take showers. And that's when the older boys took their pick of the new boys and the biggest of the older boys got first choice.

The biggest one in our dorm was Poss. He was over six feet and weighed more than two hundred pounds. First evening in the showers he walked up to me and said he wanted me to come to his bed after lights out. I said, what for, and he told me he was going to fuck me.

But the rule book they had gave us when we first got there said real plain that any boy caught doing what they called unnatural sex acts would be put in isolation and severely punished and I took that to mean that I didn't have to let Poss do what he wanted because it was against the rules so I didn't go to his bed like he told me to and he didn't come to mine.

Next day, while we was in the shop learning auto mechanics which I already knew more about than the teacher, nobody hardly talked to me. At lunch and supper breaks, Poss didn't even look at me so I reckoned that meant everything was okay. That evening, I found out how wrong I was. In the shower room six boys grabbed me and spread eagled me face down on the tile floor. One held each arm, one held each leg, and one sat in front of my face and slid forward until his hard on rubbed against my nose.

Then Poss lay down on my back and put a knife blade against my neck and said if I hollered he would cut my throat. And he made me open my mouth for the sitting boy's hard on and I felt Poss's soapy dick ram my ass. Quick as he finished another boy took his place. Then the hard on come in my mouth and as soon as I swallowed another one took its place.

Thinking back on it, I figure that in less than one hour I was gang raped by at least twenty boys and most of them took seconds in my mouth. I hadn't never felt anything like that in my life. When they finally was through with me I was so sore I couldn't move and I heard Poss tell two boys to carry me to my bunk.

Once I was there, he leaned over me and said that I had two choices. Either I could do whatever he wanted me to, whenever he wanted me to, or he would see to it I got gang raped real regular.

I could have gone to the supervisor's office next morning and reported what happened, and Poss and all the others would have been punished, and then I would have been put in what they call protective detention, which meant that every night I would be locked in one of the solitary isolation cells called the holes, where I would have been safe from any more raping. But I had heard about them holes. They was dark and damp and didn't have no running water or toilet, just a bucket, and I wouldn't have had nobody to talk to, and no radio to listen to, or nothing.

Being gang raped in the shower had made it plain to me that sex was probably the importantest thing in reform school. I learned later that they called it the pecker order, meaning the big ones fucked all the littler ones. So I decided I would be best off accepting things the way they was.

Doing anything Poss wanted would be a hell of a lot easier than getting gang raped two or three times a week or living in protective detention.

That turned out to be partly true. Poss liked to suck and he got so excited when I come in his mouth he didn't last a full minute in my ass, which I could tolerate. And he liked me to sit on the foot of his bunk and tell him stories about The Trouble Trio and he admired all I knew about cars and how things worked.

He specially liked it when I fixed an old radio that had been thrown in the trash by the supervisor's wife. It had brand new tubes, but nobody could make it work. Soon as I opened it I saw that the tuner wires was snapped. I had it fixed in ten minute and I gave it to Poss to keep next to his bed. After that, I was Poss's right hand in our dorm, and when new boys come in he sometimes shared them with me. Poss said he was partial to me because I was so little my dick looked big compared to the rest of me. Of course he was called Boss Poss Hoss, cause his cock was so damn big.

The onliest real bad problem that developed between me and Poss was that him being boss boy in our dorm he made deals with the boss boys of other dorms, trading favors for cigarettes or whatever, and one of the things boss boys traded to each other was the littler boys like me. I never knew when I was going to be told to go somewhere and strip or blow or ream or get rammed or whatever by whoever Poss had made another deal with.

If it hadn't been for that pecker order trading, I could've made out okay with life in the reformatory. As it was, things was just too rough, so I started making plans to run away. I say run away instead of escape because, like I said, there weren't hardly any guards. The doors were locked at night but leaving in the daytime would be easy as just walking away when nobody was looking. Still, I wasn't absolutely sure so I took my time getting things set up. I picked four other boys I knew was also always being traded and we decided that Sundays was the best day to run because that was visitor's day.

My Mama came to see me every Sunday that she could get my asshole stepdaddy to drive her. Sometimes one of my little half-sisters or half-brothers come with her. She always brought food; fried chicken, cornbread, one or two vegetables, ice-tea and banana pudding. My stepdaddy never came in. He stayed in the car, and when an hour had went by he started blowing the horn, meaning he was ready to leave.

It was right after one of Mama's visits, when I'd been at the reformatory just over a year, that me and them other four boys ran away, each armed with a knife stole from the mess hall.

We swore we wouldn't never be taken alive.

The next afternoon we got cornered in the woods by chain gang guards, and we was put in a dump truck, and took to Police Chief Benny Coleman's house in the town of Pamplico. He ordered us strip searched before being took back, but just when they got to me, I jumped off the truck and ran like a scalded dog. I didn't think they'd shoot me in the back and they didn't.

I made my way cross country to the hideout. Staying off the roads, it took me two days to get there. I was tired and hungry and went to sleep in the room that me and Danny and Marsh called our headquarters. I was woke up next morning by a hard kick on my butt. It was Florence County Deputy Sheriff Ray Shupe, Sr., who knew about The Hideout and figured that's where I would head.

He made me take off my clothes for a strip search and my knife fell out of my pocket. He drew his pistol and cocked it and said, "Pee Wee I could blow a hole clean through you and say you attacked me with that knife, and nobody would doubt my word. If you ever run again, you best do things a little smarter.

Then he uncocked his pistol, and I got dressed, and he handcuffed me. I was the most scared I'd ever been in my life but then Deputy Shupe acted real nice and I knew he was just trying to teach me a lesson. He even took me by his house to eat some lunch before he took me back to the reformatory.

The supervisor and superintendent was pleased to see me back but was sorely pissed off that I had chose to run away. He sentenced me to thirty strop lashes plus hard labor isolation for three months. The stropping was bad but at least it was over after a few minutes. The hard labor isolation was a hell that seemed like it wasn't never going to end. Work details started 4:30a.m., mopping the offices and classrooms, then mopping the mess hall, then cleaning the breakfast cooking pots and pans, then eating in a hurry and washing all the breakfast dishes, then peeling potatoes for lunch, then going outside to start the real hard work; digging them damned trenches.

Them trenches was the worst part of all. No matter how hot or cold, rain or dry, everyday, all day, we dug trenches four foot wide by four foot deep by one hundred foot long. When we reached the end, we went to a trench that had been dug months before and we filled it in. Soon as we got finished filling it, we were marched to a new place and started a new trench.

We was given a ten minute break every two hours for water and a piss then went back to work. If we slacked or sassed or even talked we was writ up to get strop lashes. We stopped digging a half hour for lunch then we washed all the lunch dishes, swabbed the Mess Hall, and went straight back to trench digging until supper time.

After supper we washed dishes and swabbed the mess hall again. If we didn't do a slam up job of washing and swabbing, or said anything out of line, we got writ up for that, too. By then it was usually after dark and we was marched to isolation where we had to swab the halls and clean our cells.

Then we went to the showers and when we come out we lined up naked and the guards read the list of those writ up and for what and how many strop lashes they was due. Then each one went to the hall outside the shower room and grabbed his ankles and took his strops.

And what I'm talking about wasn't just welt raising lashes. They was blood bringing whippings with an honest to god strop made from a machine drive belt. After I got writ up and stropped a few times, I learned to obey the rules.

When strop time was finished, we was give clean work clothes for the next day and a bucket for the night and went back to our cells. Lights stayed on for a half hour, but by then it was eleven or later and I was asleep on the steel cot in five minutes or less.

One Sunday a month, Mama was allowed to visit. We met in the mess hall for an hour. She could bring food to eat then and there, but she couldn't leave me nothing for later. She was also allowed to bring me paper and pencils and envelopes, but there wasn't nobody I wanted to write to.

By the time my three months was up, I was ready to get back to Poss' dorm. Anything was better than hard labor isolation. Poss said he was pissed off that I hadn't told him about my plans to escape, but he seemed happy I was back and was real nice to me the first few nights I was on his bunk. But before long he went back to trading me off to other boss boys. Some of them was even meaner than I remembered. They beat on me even when I did everything they told me to so it weren't long before I was making new plans to run away.

I made my next break with one other guy I knew I could trust. Freedom lasted six days, most of it spent in the woods in the rain, before the chain gang guards and them damn bloodhound dogs found us. When I got back to the reformatory the sentence for running away the second time was fifty strop lashes and four months hard labor isolation. By the time that was over, I was measuring them damn trenches in miles.

By the time I finally got sent back to Poss's dorm, he had done finished his time and been released and there was a new boss boy who wasn't so easy to please as Poss had been. He particularly liked to watch gang rapes with me on the bottom.

I ran away again just as soon as I could manage. It was summer and I decided the best way to do it this time was alone. I had an aunt who lived on a farm that was out of the way down in Williamsburg County, and I had got word from a cousin that she might let me stay with her in exchange for doing chores, so that was where I went and stayed for several months.

Then one Saturday my aunt went to Johnsonville to do some shopping and she come back with a distant relative of my Mama's, Weldon Parrott, who was a police officer. They both talked real nice to me for a long time and asked me lots of questions about the reformatory and when I told them about hard labor isolation and being stropped, Weldon said he wasn't going to arrest me, but he thought I ought to go back to the reformatory on my own, that he would talk to the superintendent and ask him to go easy on me if I turned myself in.

Superintendent Norman Huckabee offered me a deal; no lashes and only thirty days hard labor isolation if I came back on my own. I said that sounded fair and I went back. But as it turned out, the whole deal was bullshit. Once they had me in isolation again, I was wrote up every day and every night I got twenty lashes. After a week, the mill belt strop had cut my ass and back and legs so bad they was covered with running sores.

I complained to the night officer, Bert Calcutt, who was not much bigger than me, and asked him to let me go to the infirmary. Instead, he said he was going write me up for ten extra strop lashes for complaining. That's when that metal inside me boiled over. I hit him once in the stomach, kicked him in the balls, then kicked his face when he doubled over. He yelled for help and the other two isolation guards came and held me while he beat the hell out of me.

Next morning guards took me out of my cell and manacled me and dragged me to Superintendent Huckabee's office where I was told they was sending me to the state mental hospital on Bull Street in Columbia to have my head examined for attacking Officer Calcutt without no provocation whatsoever.

I spent five weeks locked in a solitary cell at the hospital, which looked just like a solitary cell in jail, except that the walls was painted white. The only people I saw that whole time was the orderlies who brought my food and took me to the showers once a week. Then one morning a nurse come to my cell and led me to a big office with nice furniture and I spent two hours with a man who said he was one of them psychiatrist doctors. He smoked a pipe that smelled real good and he looked up from some papers in a file folder and stared at me over the top of his wire rim glasses and didn't say nothing for the longest time. Then finally he asked me if I believed there was really a God.

I said I never had give it a whole lot of thought, but I reckoned if so many folks went to church and give their money for the Lord's work, and all such as that, there must be a God, otherwise why would they do it?

He nodded real slow and wrote something on a blue horse pad. Then he asked me if God had ever spoke to me. I said, "no, not that I recollected, not personally, anyhow."

Then he asked me if I had heard the voice of God, or any other voice, telling me to attack that girl with a hatchet. I said, "hell no! God didn't have nothing to do with it! That bitch come at me with a hatchet and I took it away from her and hit her with it to keep her from hitting me with it and that was all there were to that which was the same thing I had told to the law."

Then the Psychiatrist commenced to ask me questions about when I was little, and what happened to me then. I told him I didn't rightly remember a whole lot about them early years. Then he asked me why I reckoned it was that I couldn't remember everything that happened to me when I was a child.

And I said, as best as I was able to figure, it was probably because I had been so young at the time. truth is, I figured anything I did remember was none of his damn business, so I didn't even tell him about the carnival and the Cobra.

Then he asked me why I kept running away from reform school so I told him about the stropping and the trenches. And he said he had heard about those things before and he was sure that I understood that punishments like that was necessary for maintaining discipline, which was a real big problem at a place such as a reform school. Then we shook hands, and he said we would talk about all these things some more at my next appointment.

But we never did have no more because the very next night I got this pain in my side like somebody was squeezing my balls in a vise and I started vomiting and yelling and finally an orderly come to see about me, and he called a nurse, and they took me to the infirmary, then to a real hospital where they operated on me because I had a ruptured appendix.

When I got well enough, they sent me back to the reformatory with instructions I was to be on light duty for three months. The only reason I could figure why they didn't send me back to the mental hospital was that somebody screwed up and lost my paperwork. In the years ahead I found out that things like that happen a lot to inmates and their records.

At any rate, whatever the reason, I was just as happy not to get sent back to the nut house to see that psychiatrist doctor again and have to answer his crazy ass questions. At the reformatory they kept me in an isolation cell day and night. After two months of solitary the thought of digging trenches started appealing to me. At the end of three months, I was told they was planning to send me out again with the work crews.

Then this new night officer named M.F. Quick come to me and said that because of what I had done to his friend, Officer Calcutt, he was going to write me up for ten strop lashes every night after showers as soon as I was back on labor detail whether I done anything to deserve being writ up or not.

I figured I was fucked no matter what, so the day I went back to work I waited until I was sent out of the mess hall to clean garbage barrels, then I made a run for the hedges and kept on going. I went to Sumter, a town not too far away from Florence. Poss had told me he stayed there with his uncle who put together crews to work carnivals and they weren't too particular about who they hired.

I found Poss's uncle and I found Poss and I got a job being what they called a roustabout, helping setup and take down. But my side where I had had the rupturing appendix give me trouble. I got a hernia from all the heavy lifting. So Poss's uncle, a hell of a good man who reminded me a lot of Danny's daddy, got me a job night watching the office wagons.

We traveled a route down through Florida, then back up through Georgia to North Carolina. It was my first growed up freedom and I sure did like it. When we got back to Sumter, I had to be careful where I went. It was 1950, and I was an escapee from reform school trying to figure what to do next. I damn sure didn't want to get spotted and picked up by the law so I laid low at Poss's uncle's house and hardly never went anywhere except occasionally with Poss to one little town or another to do some shopping or see a movie or eat a burger.

It was during them times that I met Mary. She was thirteen and a half years old and the most beautiful girl I ever seen in my life. When I was around her, I felt like a combination of a lamb who couldn't bleat and a rhino with a four foot hard on. I begged her to marry me. She said she didn't want to be married to a boy who couldn't even walk down Main Street with her because the law was looking for him. She said I should go back to reform school and finish my sentence, which was just a few more months, then I would be free to lead a normal free life with a wife. But she said she wanted it understood real clear between us that she wasn't never going to travel with no carnival. She wanted a home, and husband, and children. If she couldn't have all three she would do without any until the right man come along.

I married Mary on January 22, 1951 and spent one night with her before I surrendered to Johnsonville police officer Clinton Gaskins, who was kin to my real daddy, and he took me back to reform school.

Superintendent Huckabee said no lashes, no hard labor, just an isolation cell twenty-four hours a day for the three months remaining on my sentence, except for my one morning walk to take a shower and empty my shit bucket.

I guess that was when I first started reading serious things like magazines, and newspapers, and books. Mary brought them to me. I was allowed to see her every Sunday for an hour in the visitor's room of the isolation building. That hour was what I lived for. That hour and knowing that every Sunday meant one less week until I was out and with her.

I was feeling so good, I decided it would be fun to try to drive the isolation guards crazy. When I had worked night watching with the carnival, it was my job to carry a ring of keys and check all the doors to the concession wagons. In the process of doing that, I got interested in how locks worked and before long I could take them apart and put them back together. I wasn't no first class locksmith, but I knowed a lot about what a key did to make a lock open.

When I was put back in reform school isolation I looked at the lock on my cell door and realized I could open that one with my belt buckle. So every evening when the guards came in with the work details, I would be out of my cell, sitting in the hallway or taking a shower. And after lights out, I opened all the cells on the block and let the other guys out and we sat in the corridors and shot the shit. On their rounds, the guards would hear us and come in and put us all back in our cells and on next rounds we would be out again.

The officers questioned everybody on isolation, and all they would say was, "Pee Wee lets us out," which is what I had told them to say.

finally Superintendent Huckabee called me to his office and agreed to let me out of isolation for the rest of my sentence if I would stop opening the cells and if I would tell him how I did it. I wouldn't agree until he gave me a note in writing saying what I was supposed to do for him and what he was going to do in return. I wanted to make sure that this deal worked better than the last one

I made with him. This time he kept his word.

Of course, the record keepers fucked up my paperwork, so it was three weeks later than it was supposed to be when I finally got out. On release day, Mary, and Mama, and my stepdaddy come to get me. I was a free man with a loving wife and there weren't no lawmen looking to put me back in jail.

I aimed to keep it that way.

4

The only work I could find around Florence was day labor on a construction job, which mostly meant pushing a wheelbarrow and toting heavy stuff like bricks and shingles. What I really wanted to do was work on cars, but there just weren't any jobs. Seemed like everybody who was in World War Two had learned to be a mechanic in the Army. Or at least that's what they told me when I applied for work, though I suspected that the fact I had just got out of reform school for using a hatchet on that girl was the real reason nobody was exactly eager to hire me.

I took shade tree repair work on weekends but couldn't make near enough at that and day laboring to support me and Mary. I was real discouraged, and to top it off, Mary got pregnant. Having a baby was something we both wanted, but it meant I needed real bad to make more money.

I thought about taking up doing breaking and entering again, but I knew the law was keeping eyes on me, besides which I didn't have any fencing connections. Poss had gone on the road full time with the carnival, and I flat didn't know anybody else I could trust. All the boys who hung out at the hideout when we was younger had growed up, got married, and straightened.

Trying to find some better work and pay, Mary and me moved from Florence to Georgetown, on the coast, where we lived with some of her kin, but nobody didn't need mechanics there neither, so I ended up working for some men who had a government contract to log cypress in the swamps of the Little Pee Dee River in Horry County, which is most famous for being the county where

Myrtle Beach is located.

It was damn hard work, as hard or harder than digging trenches. I spent the whole day up to my ass in slimy water, being bit by mosquitos and gnats and no-see-ums, and jumping out of the way every time a snake fell from a tree or swum by. Summer heat and sweat made it even worse.

The only good thing was the pay. I took home more money than I ever had before. That was when I started stopping most nights at a honkytonk called the House of Blue Lights. I never was much of a drinking man, two beers was about all I could ever handle, but I do like them honkytonk women and listening to Hank on the jukebox and swapping stories with good old boys.

Nobody bothered to let me know that the logging company's contract wouldn't last but a few weeks. I didn't find out about that until I got my final pay slip. Suddenly I was out of a job, looking for work again for the fourth time in the six months since I had got out of the reformatory.

Me and Mary moved back to Florence where still the onliest work I could find was part time construction labor. I didn't mind working my ass off, even in snaky swamps, if the money was good, but damned if I could stand doing shit work for hardly no pay. I knew there had to be a better and easier way.

Then one evening at a roadhouse outside Florence, I met up with a fellow I recognized from reform school. They called him The Slick Duck from the way he greased down his hair and brushed it to a duck's ass in the back. I didn't hardly really know Slick, he had got released just a few weeks after I arrived at the reformatory and we wasn't in the same dorm, and Poss didn't never trade me to him, but we vaguely remembered one another by sight. He told me he had served two years hard time in the penitentiary since then for aggravated assault, and he damn sure didn't recommend prison cause it was a whole shit pot worse than reform school.

We laughed and talked a long time like we was old friends, then he said that if I was looking for work he could give me a job. He had a labor contract, hiring and overseeing harvesters and graders and hanger workers for three big tobacco planters. I told him I had growed up on tobacco farms and knew a lot about grading and hanging, but that I truly hated farm work. He said I should take the job anyhow then gave me a cigar and a beer and a wink, and I knew there was more to his offer than just farming.

Slick got us a house rent free on a farm near Kingsbrough Crossroads which is a few miles out of Johnsonville on Highway Fifty-One. It was three rooms and outdoor plumbing, but there was electric lights and a well pump. I was relying heavy on Stick's promise there would be better money before too long.

Mary learned tobacco grading real fast. At first, I worked mostly at hanging, until Slick realized I knew as much about motors as I claimed I did, then he had me work on the old stake body trucks they used for hauling. Every Saturday Mary and me drew down fifteen dollars each against what would be our due when the crop was in and we drove into Florence in one of the trucks Slick said we could use. Almost always we went to see a movie then did some shopping for ourselves and the baby we expected in the spring. After we bought groceries for the coming week, we was damn lucky to have enough left to pay the electricity bill.

Late one Saturday, after I had been working there a couple of months, Slick picked me up in his '50 Chevy and we drove for two hours to a big tobacco barn way out in the middle of nowhere. Some black field hands was there with four empty trucks waiting for us. We went through the barn taking the best tobacco out and putting it on the trucks, which was then drove away. Then Slick and me sat in his car for a long time. He said we was keeping watch in case anybody happened to come by, but nobody did. At just past midnight we went into the barn and stacked loose tobacco against the wood walls and set it on fire. It don't take kerosene, or gasoline, or paint thinner, or any other kind of starter to set that barn a blazing. Tobacco is its own best fuel.

The whole sky was lit up so bright we could still see it glowing above the pine trees when we was five miles away. Slick drove me home and gave me three hundred dollars cash. I didn't ask questions, I just said thank you and went inside and gave the Money to Mary then spent the rest of the night trying to convince her I hadn't stole it. I told her it was a bonus for our good work. I never did tell her about burning barns, though I think she figured it out because whenever I was gone most of the night there was news of barn fires on the radio the next day.

But there wasn't no way the law could ever prove arson unless somebody talked and I knew Slick wouldn't talk and he knew I wouldn't talk, and we never give a thought to any of them hands talking. In those days, in that part of the South, black people knew that black people who talked too much didn't live real long.

Slick and me burned two more barns in South Carolina and three in North Carolina before Christmas. By then I had almost two thousand dollars stashed from burnings. That was a hell of a lot of money in 1951. On top of that, me and Mary had nearly five hundred more that was paid us as our due after deducting our draw for the work on the farm. Far as I was concerned, comparing what I got for barn burning to what we got for damn near a year's work just proved what I already knew, that there was more money to be made illegally than any job ever paid.

I bought a Chevy that spring. To be precise, I bought it the week before our baby daughter was born on April 17, 1952. It was near planting time. I signed on with Slick for another year of keeping the equipment running, and we started our draw for the new season at sixteen dollars a week each instead of fifteen. That spring I also did my first not tobacco barn burning. It was a warehouse and I got paid almost a thousand dollars for doing it because going into Charlotte to burn a building was a whole lot riskier than setting fire to a barn out in the country.

It was while we was driving back home after the burning that night that Slick explained to me that not only was them tobacco barns we had burned insured for the value of the buildings, more than enough to build brand new barns, the tobacco in them had been inspected and certified, so federal government insurance paid off the crop loss at season prices.

Of course, that tobacco hadn't really been burned at all, it had been hauled across state lines and sold at auction through other farmers who were in on the scam. But Slick made it a point to be real clear in telling me that the farmers he had work contracts with, like the one whose land me and Mary lived on and we worked for, wasn't a part of what was going on and didn't know nothing about the torching and reselling. Slick used their trucks and paid some of their hands to help out, but the burning we done was far away from Florence County.

After Slick explained all that to me I started wondering why, if there was enough money being made from burning tobacco barns to make it worth the risk for the planters and to make it possible for Slick to own a '50 Chevy and a new house, how come I could only afford an old '39 and still had to go to the outhouse to take a shit. But I kept my thoughts to myself through planting season and in to that summer when we torched another warehouse and two more curing barns.

Most Friday and Saturday nights me and Slick went to the honkytonks looking for action. He drank and got loud. I drove and laughed a lot. We went as far as Charleston and Columbia, like me, and Marsh, and Danny had used to do, and once when we was in a bar near the docks in Charleston, Slick got real drunk and, in front of two girls we was talking to, he bet me ten dollars I wouldn't go in the back room and get tattooed.

I won that bet right quick. I got the words Pee Wee writ on my shoulder. The girls watched and got such sticky crotches they could hardly wait to get to our room. Slick said lots of women got turned slimy by tattoos. That may be true, I can't say for sure because that was the onliest time I ever got one out on the streets. I did get a skull put on my other shoulder years later when I was in CCI. But before long I sure wished I hadn't never gotten that one in Charleston.

That summer I couldn't get thoughts about the money from barn burning off my mind. Every week I decided I ought to have a face off with Slick and demand a bigger share but for one reason or another I didn't get around to it and like some other times in my life I waited too long.

The law come to our house before dawn one Monday morning. Mary and me was still in bed. The deputies was politer than most, they said they wasn't looking for me, just thought I might know where Slick was.

I told them that if he weren't at his house, I didn't have no idea of his whereabouts, that him and me had been out to have a beer on Saturday night but I hadn't seen him since, which was true. I was scared shitless they was after him for arson and he might name me to lighten his own load. So I was truly surprised when I asked, calm as I could, why they was looking for Slick, and they told me that his ex-wife and her new husband, who lived in Charleston, had been killed Sunday about supper time and Slick had been seen going in their house right before gunshots was heard and his two little bitty kids who were there said their daddy had shot their mommy and stepdaddy.

It was pretty obvious to me right then and there that Slick wasn't going to be coming back to his contract on that tobacco farm ever again. I kept doing my work, waiting for some news. Three days later it was on the radio that Stick's car had been found in Alabama, but the law didn't have a clue where he had gone from there.

A week later a fellow named Arthur Lewis, who was one of the men I had worked for in Horry County when he had that government cypress logging business, come by my house to let me know that he had took over Slick's contract and was now in charge of tobacco operations for the land-owners. He said that me and Mary could stay on, but there wouldn't be no draws anymore, just a settlement at season's end. However, there was going to be more logging work later in the year and I could have a job there after the end of tobacco season.

I still had most of my burning money stashed away so I wasn't hurting for cash and I said okay. Then, like things wasn't already turning to shit and trouble fast enough, a whole new pot full was dumped on me just a few days before settle up and season end. Two teenage girls who lived on the farm come walking into a hanging barn where I was working on the curing racks and they started talking real nasty to me. They was always ragging at me about something, calling me names and what not like they was better than me and Mary.

I told them to leave me alone, I didn't want no trouble with them, I was busy. That's when the older one, who had a real shit spout for a mouth, said she had heard her daddy and some others talking about me having something to do with burning a tobacco barn and they was just waiting for settle up day to have me arrested so they wouldn't have to pay me any share for my work. Then she said that I wasn't nothing but scum and ought to be sent to the chain gang where I belonged.

Right away the metal in my gut started burning and rolling. The more she said the hotter it got. I told her to shut the fuck up and get the hell away from me, but instead of listening to what I said, she walked up closer and said she had a mind to tell her daddy I had grabbed her and kissed her and tried to rape her just to make real sure I went to prison for a long time or at least got the hell beat out of me.

Then she spit at me and said, "but you ain't worth the trouble, Pee Wee. You ain't even good enough to kiss my ass."

I swung the ballpeen hammer I had been using to shape a flue and hit her just behind her right ear. It made a popping sound, like wood cracking. Then I smacked her again, this time on top of her head, and she fell to the barn floor and didn't move. I kicked her in the face just for good measure.

The other girl screamed and ran like hell. I started to chase her, then decided it might be smarter to put some distance between me and that barn before the other girl came back with a whole mess of daddies and the law.

I hated that I didn't have time to go explain to Mary what had happened, but at least she knew where I kept our cash, so she and the baby wouldn't go hungry and homeless. I didn't take the car. I would be too easy spotted driving my own car. I took one of the stake body trucks and left.

I abandoned the truck on the other side of Johnsonville not far from Leo and Prospect and made my way through woods and across fields to the Johnsonville American Legion Hut and hid there. The hut was only used for Legion meetings and some special occasions, and it was situated so I could spot anybody coming and get out the back way. I broke into the vending machines and lived on soft drinks and candy and crackers. I put the coins from the machines in a sack with cigarettes, crackers, candy and gum, just in case I had to leave in a hurry.

I had started smoking not long after I quit school, but I hadn't never bought more than one pack at a time, except when I was honkytonking, them women always expected the men to furnish the beer, the smokes and the rubbers.

Nobody came looking for me at the Legion Hut. I could have stayed there longer, but after a few days I started feeling like somebody had locked me inside a cage and I couldn't get out. It was like the building got littler and littler the longer I was there. I felt like I was smothering to death. So to show my appreciation for using the hut to hide out, I set it on fire and left.

Two nights later I was sleeping in a deserted tenant shack when the law surrounded it and called me out. One deputy fired two shots that ricocheted off the chimney, just to let me know they meant business. I got their message and surrendered.

The prosecutor charged me with attempted murder, and assault with a deadly weapon with intent to inflict grave bodily harm, and arson for setting fire to the Legion Hut. Nothing was ever mentioned about me burning tobacco farms.

They tried me first on the arson charge but the onliest evidence the deputies had against me was their claim that they had followed a trail of chewing gum and candy wrappers from the Legion Hut to the tenant house where they captured me.

The court appointed lawyer who defended me put me on the stand and I admitted I had served time in reform school and that I was running from the law when I got caught, but I swore, like I had to my lawyer, that I had been staying in a barn near our old hideout and hadn't been near the Legion Hut. The jury believed me, like my lawyer did, because I didn't deny I was on the run for an attempted murder. They figured, like I knew they would, that if I admitted that, why would I lie about the arson?

They acquitted me. Mary was as happy as I was, but I wouldn't let her use our savings to put up bail for me so the Sheriff locked me up to wait for my next trial. Mary brought fried chicken and biscuits to me at the jail almost every evening.

A few days after my first trial ended Solicitor J. Ruben Long came to my cell with my lawyer and said that if I would plead guilty to the lesser charge of assault and battery, he would drop the attempted murder and intent to kill parts of the charge and get the judge to give me just eighteen months. True, I had fractured the bitch's skull, but there is a difference, my lawyer said, in injury inflicted in the heat of passion and injury inflicted deliberately and intentionally, and the Solicitor would have a hard time proving that I intended to kill her. My lawyer recommended I take the deal. I agreed that it seemed like a good idea. But I fucked up. I didn't get the deal in writing.

Next morning, they took me before judge T.B. Greniker. He asked how I pleaded. I didn't wait for my lawyer, I said, "guilty, your honor."

And he said, "your plea is accepted and I hereby sentence you to the South

Carolina State Penitentiary in Columbia for a period of five years."

My lawyer said, "five years? Your Honor, our plea bargain deal with Solicitor Long was for eighteen months."

The judge said, "after reviewing the evidence, I have rejected that agreement. The sentence stands. Five years."

I said, "well fuck you, you old son of a bitch!"

judge Greniker banged his gavel. "That will be one additional year for contempt."

I shut up and turned around and looked at Mary and our baby. They was both crying.

5

When me and Marsh and Danny use to go to the Saturday afternoon movies our favorites were the ones with Jimmy Cagney, and George Raft, and Edward G. Robinson. Those were truly fine men that a kid could look up to. They was tough and didn't take no shit off nobody, but they was always loyal to one another and they almost always ended up getting sent up the river to the big house with its high walls, and towers, and fog always covering over everything.

That was exactly what the South Carolina State Penitentiary, The pen, looked like when I saw it that first time in the fall of 1952. It was the dreariest looking place on earth, setting there like a dungeon castle on the side of the river marshes at Columbia. And there weren't no kindly Pat O'Brien around, there was just tough ass guards carrying nightsticks, they called them billy clubs back then, that was lathed down hardwood two by fours. Everything was strict discipline. The warden made the rules, the guards saw to it that inmates obeyed them and did like they was told. Guards was called Mister and Sir and if an inmate stepped out of line he got whacked. If he did it too often he got the shit beat out of him and throwed in solitary.

I don't mind admitting that when I first got there, I was plenty scared. Every time we went to the showers I expected to be spread eagled face down and raped. But that didn't never happen. Instead, for the first few weeks hardly none of the other inmates said a word to me. I was in a two man cell but didn't have no cellmate. When I spoke to anybody in the yard they turned and walked away like I wasn't there. And there was a no talking rule in the mess hall so I didn't dare try to start up a conversation there.

This was a lot different from reform school. This was the big house, The pen, with tiers of cells, bars everywhere, and constant noise. But the worse part was not knowing what was going to happen next.

And it was the first time I had ever seen black inmates. There hadn't been none at reform school. There was a separate reformatory for them, and I had thought there was separate prison for them too or that they was all kept on chain gangs, but I was wrong. There was blacks in the pen, only they was locked up in different buildings from whites. Separate but equal is what the law was said, which meant that in the mess hall the blacks had their own line and the tables where they ate was partitioned off from ours, but their food and ours was equally shitty.

When I got to the pen, first off they put me to work on the kitchen crew, washing pots and pans, and mopping floors. I found out later that that was where everybody started. Trusties, inmates trusted with more freedoms and privileges, ran the kitchen and reported to the guards what they thought of the new inmates, whether they worked hard and took orders and didn't break rules and all that. Based on what the trusties reported, the inmate was given his permanent job after a month. I went from the kitchen to the laundry then later to the garages to work on prison trucks and machines of all kinds.

It was while I was on kitchen duty and nobody was having nothing to do with me that I got the feeling there was somebody else besides trusties watching and making up their minds about me. It figured that the pen had its own pecker order, like reform school, only I didn't have any idea what the rules were, and nobody would tell me. I learned later that the idea was to make new meat like me be so scared and unsure that we would accept anything that happened to us. And believe me, it worked.

The first contact I got was when a crew cut guy with biceps big as my thighs came up to me in the yard and offered me a cigarette and then, real casual, told me that from now on I belonged to Arthur and he nodded in the direction of a group of older men about fifty feet away. He explained that them older inmates were the power men of the pen and they got first choice of the new meat. What they didn't want, the others could fight over. Nobody did nothing, he said, unless the power men said it was okay. And Arthur, who was one of the powerfullest, had decided he wanted me to be his boy, his cellmate, under his protection. In other words, his personal property.

If I didn't like the idea, I could ask for protective custody and spend my six year sentence in solitary. It was like reform school all over again. But I actually felt kind of relieved. At least now I knew what to expect.

That evening the guards transferred me to Arthur's cell. He reminded me of my stepdaddy. He didn't say hey or anything. He just told me to strip and when I did he kicked me in the balls, he still had his shoes on. Then he proceeded to beat me with his fists. He blacked my eyes, bloodied my nose, then held me face down on the cement floor and choked me while he fucked me. He was big and he took a real long time and it hurt bad. Afterwards he made me lick him clean.

For the next six months I did whatever Arthur said, for him or anybody he gave me to. Problem was, the other power men he traded me to weren't just interested in fucking and sucking, they all liked it rough and there were times I thought I was going to have my balls smashed or my dick cut off and be left to bleed to death in a laundry room or storage closet. I had gone from being what they called new meat to one of the nobodies, young, too small to fight back, available for them to play with, beat on, torture, or even kill.

The power men controlled everything and had all kinds of deals working for them so even if they did kill another inmate and got caught, which weren't likely cause nobody would dare rat them out, they would most likely get another life sentence which didn't mean shit to them.

They were the most violentest men I had ever been around. They ran the inside of the prison by their own rules and the guards overlooked most of the rules they broke because the power men helped them keep order and sometimes traded favors with them. Like Slick said, prison was a whole shit pot worse than reform school. And no matter how much I wanted to I couldn't just run-away. Planning an escape from The pen would take a long time, and even the best plan I could come up with might not be successful. But by the end of six months I knew I had to do something and I had to do it soon. I had had all that I could take.

I decided that if I couldn't figure a way to escape maybe I should try to become a power man. That would sure make things better, though it didn't seem too likely that I was suddenly going to get big enough even to defend myself, much less beat up on others. All I knew, there had to be something I could do.

I gave it lots of thought and I reckoned that I needed to come up with an act so goddamned violent that every man in The pen would be scared shitless of me and what I might do next. And the onliest way to do that was to make my bones. I had to kill somebody, and not just anybody, I had to kill somebody powerful and special.

I hadn't really never give much thought to what killing a man meant or what it might be like. I never did a whole lot of thinking about what things meant. I usually just made up my mind what needed doing then proceeded to plan on doing it. I had heard Arthur and some of the others say that the meanest inmate in the whole prison was Hazel Brazell, who nobody dared to call by anything except his last name, Brazell. It was easy to see that everybody, including Arthur, was scared shitless of him.

Brazell stayed mostly to himself. He had his boys and he didn't do much trading. Usually, he just said what he wanted and got it and didn't give nothing in return, which didn't set too well with the power men who had their own rules about what was fair trade and what not.

One night during my seventh month there, when Arthur had finished with me and seemed real calm, I told him I had heard lots of talk about Brazell not abiding by trading rules and cheating other power men and having his boys steal from them and all kinds of things like that and I wondered why they had let him get away with it all them years, why nobody had killed him yet. Anybody else who did what Brazell done would be found in the shower one night hanging from a pipe. It seemed to me, I said, that letting Brazell get away with all the things he had done was just setting a bad example.

Arthur laughed, which was one of the few times I ever heard him laugh without somebody else screaming in pain, and he said that Brazell couldn't be got to. His boys were the biggest and toughest there were and he let them be as mean as they wanted to be just so they protected him. That was how come nobody could get close enough to Brazell to even touch him, much less kill him.

I said, "I figure anybody can be got to. I know I could kill him."

Arthur said, "Pee Wee, you couldn't kill a green fly stuck on a horse turd."

I didn't say nothing back. I just stretched out on my cot and closed my eyes, but I didn't sleep at all that night. I had plans that needed plotting. Inside of three days I knew what Brazell liked to eat and drink, and what his schedule was, and everything else I needed to know about him and his boys.

I went to the kitchen and told the head trustee that Arthur wanted a ham and cheese sandwich, and while he was making it I slipped a short paring knife from the counter into my pocket. Then I went to the canteen and got a Orange Crush and I walked to Brazell's block straight to his cell. He was lying on his cot looking at a magazine, two of his boys was on the tier outside his cell, another one was inside with him. I held out the sandwich and drink and said real loud that this was from Arthur. He didn't say nothing, just nodded, and his boys let me walk in and put the food on the table by his cot.

Over the next couple of weeks, I did the same thing three more times, looking over the situation, working on a plan, and figuring my odds. When I went to Brazell's cell the fifth time, I plain got lucky. Only one of his boys was around, standing on the tier outside his cell door and Brazell wasn't on his cot reading or taking a nap like he did most midafternoons, he was naked, sitting on the toilet.

I told his boy that I had a sandwich and drink for Brazell from Arthur who wanted to set a time to come over to discuss something with Brazell, if Brazell would see him. The boy asked Brazell if he should let me come in the cell. Brazell farted real loud and grunted, "yeah, let the little piss ant in," then motioned me to put the sandwich and drink on the table and said for me to tell Arthur to come over that evening during free time after supper.

I put the food down, palmed the knife from my pocket and took two steps to the toilet. Brazell was reading a magazine. He looked up at me and said, "what the fuck you staring at?"

I didn't hesitate a lick. I jabbed the knife into his left juggler vein and sliced toward his Adam's apple, then twisted it deep in his pulse artery. Brazell's throat was cut open before he could raise his arms to protect himself. He tried to yell but just gurgled.

I surprised myself at how calm I was. I didn't really feel nothing much at all. I watched the way the blood spurts got shorter and shorter until finally they just ran down his chest and gut to his crotch. Then he slumped sideways and fell off the toilet.

His boy rushed inside the cell, shank in hand. I held up the paring knife and said, you're crazy as shit if you fight me over a man who's already dead. Now go call the guards."

I waited on Brazell's cot until they arrived and cuffed me. Then I stood between two guards until the captain and the warden got there which was about twenty minutes later. They asked me lots of questions, but all I would say was that me and Brazell had got in a argument and I killed him.

The warden ordered me took to solitary.

In prison, word spreads faster than a fart in church. By the time the guards walked me down the steps and outside across the yard to the maximum security building, inmates was lined up on the tiers and I could hear them saying my name. They arrested Arthur and put him in solitary confinement, too. The warden said that Arthur must have ordered me to kill Brazell so they charged us both with murder.

I figured that Arthur would be so damn mad about that that my life wouldn't be worth green apple splatters. But when they took us both to the conference room to wait for the lawyers assigned to defend us, Arthur smiled and gave me a big hug and congratulated me for having the balls to kill Brazell. With him gone, Arthur was the number one power in the prison and he said that as far as he was concerned, I was second only to him.

I felt great. I had done it. I wasn't never going to be nobody's boy again. And like that wasn't enough good luck, when our lawyers arrived with the solicitor they all agreed that if anybody in the South Carolina State Penitentiary deserved killing, it was Brazell.

We cut a deal which was put it in writing. Me and Arthur both plea bargained to manslaughter. The judge gave Arthur fifteen years concurrent with the life sentence he was serving, which would still make him eligible for parole in ten years and the judge gave me nine years, six concurrent with the six I was already serving, which meant just three extra years.

I figured that was a damn fair deal, considering I wouldn't never again have to be afraid of anybody in The pen no matter how long I was there. I was in solitary for six weeks. When I got put back into the general population, I had my own boy to wash my clothes. I never hurt him. I never traded him to nobody. And whenever another power man sent someone special to me or I got money or cigarettes, I shared with him. I always treated him like I wished Poss and Arthur and others had treated me.

After I was sentenced for Brazell's murder all the inmates and guards looked at me different. Making my bones had made my reputation. I was a killer, not to be fucked with, no matter my size.

My new power made 1953 and 1954 as tolerable as any two years in prison could possibly be. I did truly believe that everything was going to be okay for the next five years, which was when I was due to come up for parole. Then, just like it had done before, trouble sneaked up behind me and bit me on the ass.

Inside The pen, I could handle anything that happened. I was ready and willing to do whatever needed doing, including killing again. But this trouble come from the streets outside and it flat tore me apart and frustrated the hell out of me because I couldn't do a goddamned thing about it.

In the middle of 1953, Mary divorced me.

6

When I learnt Mary was getting a divorce there wasn't no way I could stay in prison. Don't get me wrong, I didn't want to get out so I could do her harm. I loved Mary and our little girl too much to ever hurt them. But Mary had made it real plain to me that there wasn't no sense in her and me talking about us ever being together any more. Her mind was made up. We was finished. And that made me hurt so much that me having everything just like I wanted it in the penitentiary weren't enough anymore. I needed real bad to get back out on the streets again.

I knew my chances of escaping was skinny as a coon dick toothpick, but I kept looking for a way and working on a plan. That was all I thought about day and night, and like everything else I ever set my mind to do, I did it.

I escaped from the South Carolina State Penitentiary in 1955 hidden on the back of a prison garbage truck. Several other inmate mechanics who worked in the garage wanted to escape with me, but I told them we couldn't all just pile in the back of the truck and wave at the tower guards as we rode out. I said that anybody who wanted in on my plan had to be able to fit inside one of them garbage drums that was carried in back of the truck to be put out to replace the full cans of garbage picked up.

It turned out, like I knew it would, that I was the onliest one little enough to get inside one of the drums and the lid be put back on. They was some real disappointed men. It was the first time I ever saw anybody envy me being so little, but, to their credit, even though none of them could go with me, they all helped me pull it off. We drilled three one inch holes in the drum two in the lid for air and one in the side so I could look out and see if a guard or anybody got in the back of the truck. When the driver and his helper, both trusties who were in on the plan because they couldn't dare say no to me without committing suicide, came to get the truck right after lunch, I was already inside the drum. The lid was on tight, but I could knock it loose whenever I wanted to get out. I had thought through my plan real thorough. That's another advantage us inmates have, the officials and guards have to think about all the details of running the prison and keeping track of hundreds of inmates while the inmates don't have nothing to think about except finding a way to get out.

I knew I wouldn't be missed until bed check. The men in the mechanic garage usually worked right up to supper time and went straight to the mess hall, except that if we wanted, we was allowed to go straightaway to the canteen and get sandwiches instead so the guards didn't take no notice if we weren't in line or at a mess hall table. Then all the inmates had free time for two hours after supper for visiting other cells or playing cards and such unless they had been writ up for rule breaking and were doing punishment detail work like kitchen duty or mopping or something. At the end of free time there was a half hour for showers before we were whistled into our cells and the tier trusties closed and locked down the doors. Once we was in for the night, the guards made bed check. It was usually about nine o'clock by then, but if things went like I planned, I would have done gone out the prison front gate sometime between three and four.

Even though it was cool weather, I sweated liked a fresh cut boar hog while the truck made its way to all the buildings in the prison complex, picking up and putting out cans. It was near three p.m. when I heard guards' voices and knew we were at the gate. I could see one uniform climb into the back of the truck, but he didn't stay too long. The smell had got a lot worse after the pickup of drums of rotten food from back of the mess hall. I couldn't blame the guard for not inspecting every barrel, which was something else I had counted on. The back of that truck stank so bad that if I hadn't had such a damn good reason to stay, I would have got off myself.

The truck made four more stops for gates to be opened then it picked up speed and rolled along pretty good for about twenty minutes before it stopped and the driver banged the top of the cab three times to signal me that we had left the main highway near the county dump and everything was clear.

I popped the lid off my metal drum, hoisted myself out, stretched the cramps from my legs, looked to see for myself that there wasn't nobody else around, then I jumped off the rear of the truck. The driver didn't wait, soon as he saw me in his rear view mirror he put it in low and drove away.

When the driver was questioned later about my escape, which I new he surely would be because he had driven from the prison in a truck that had spent the morning in the garage where I worked, he would say that he didn't have no idea how I had escaped, but it surely weren't in his truck. All them barrels was empty when he started his route, and a guard inspected the whole load when he stopped at the front gate and the truck was unloaded at the dump by landfill workers.

My plan worked because nobody who knew anything dared to talk. Power men inside saw to that, and years later people still was always asking me how I did it. And I always just smiled and never told them, until now.

Of course getting off the garbage truck near the Columbia-Florence highway didn't mean I was safe. I was out, but I wouldn't be free until I put a hell of a lot of miles between me and prison. And I couldn't just flag down a bus or hitch a ride. So I did what was natural for me, I headed into the woods and cross country toward Leo and Lake City and Johnsonville.

Like I said, I didn't plan on going looking for Mary and I sure wasn't stupid enough to head back to the Hideout or my Mama's house. I headed to that general area because that's where I knew everybody and the kind of car they owned and where they parked it, and where the keys probably was, and when the owners slept, and most likely who with and knowing all that was important because the next step in my plan was to steal a car. I ended up going into Lake City and stealing one from my cousin, David Gaskins, who owned the Peppermint Gas Station.

A week later I was in Lake Wales, Florida. I didn't go there by chance neither. I hadn't stayed in contact with Poss, but I knowed that the carnival kept pretty much the same schedule every year. That being true, the would be in Florida getting set for the road tour to commence. I found Poss living in a trailer south of Orlando. He was married with three kids and a wife who had told him she was sick and tired of doing the carny circuit ten months a year. She wanted a house without any goddamn wheels on it. She was the unpleasantest part of my stay. She bitched the whole time so I tried to be extra nice to her specially when Poss and me wanted to go out for a few beers. We needed time to ourselves. We had lots of catch up talking to do to get to know one another again.

I wasn't too worried that he might drop a dime on me, but just to be sure, I told him right off that I had been in The pen, and made my bones while I was there, then escaped. Poss specially liked it that I had become a killer. He couldn't wait to tell his wife and she suddenly quit her bitching and started being real polite to me. Then I told her that my ex-wife Mary had felt the same way she did about carnival living, and she beamed her pleasure.

When I told Poss right in front of her that I agreed with her and thought he ought to save up and buy a real house for her and the kids, Poss looked at me like I was treasoning him by siding with her. Then I said that in order to save money Poss ought to leave his wife and kids where they were and go on the carny road alone and send her money to live on and put in a savings account for a real house. Poss caught my stream real quick. By the time we left to go on the road with the carnival, Poss's wife and Poss was real happy, and they both thought I was some kind of saint.

But before long I knew that carnival life just wasn't right for me anymore. Grant you, it's a good world to live in when you're on the run, howsomever, I was older and smarter than that boy who ran away from reform school and was grateful for any help of any kind from just about anybody. Now I needed to make more than minimum wages as a roustabout or security night watchman.

Poss had his own ring toss concession on the midway and his hustle was pretty good but he couldn't afford to pay for his new girlfriend plus send money to his wife and kids plus pay me to work for him so I had to do whatever work I could get.

I operated the ferris wheel and the octopus ride when the owner was too busy or too drunk to do it and, since we took all the rides apart every time we moved the midway to a new town, learning how they worked and how to repair them was easy. Trouble was, damn near all the carny workers knew as much or more than I did about how to work on them.

I never made any decent money until I got to know the man and wife who owned the girlie show. He bought and sold guns as a sideline, and he taught me how to rebuild pieces, weapons, I mean. I didn't need teaching how to work on the pieces in his show. And every once in a while, he had a car he wanted stripped. His brother brought in the cars. I took them apart in a tent behind the girlie show trailer. His brother picked up the filed parts and towed away the chassis when he brought the next car. That kept me pretty busy and put some good cash in my pockets.

The worst enemy the carnival had was rain. When it poured down, the midway closed. If it happened on say a Thursday, and no letup was forecast soon, everything closed for the rest of the week and me and Poss drove in my car, the one I had stole from my cousin, to visit his wife and kids while his girlfriend drove his truck and trailer to the next setup.

It was on one of those trips to Lake Wales that Poss's wife introduced me to a friend of hers named Junie Alice Holden. I don't know what got into me, but every time I was around that girl my balls and pecker felt like a nest full of hornets was inside buzzing around and stinging and trying to shoot out.

She was nineteen and knew what was what, but she wouldn't do nothing to ease my pain. The onliest way I could get her to relieve my condition was to marry her. I left Poss to get back to the carnival the best way he could and I took off with Junie.

We got married and stayed together two weeks before I ran out of money and all them hornets suddenly either died in their nest or had flew out my pee hole and drowned in her pussy. I knew right then that there weas no way our marriage was ever going to work. I took her back home to Lake Wales and I went back to the carnival and I never saw her again.

When I wasn't working car stripping I spent less and less time with Poss, who was royally pissed at me for running off and leaving him to hitch from Lake Wales for the setup in Valdosta. That was when I started spending more and more time with one of the girlie show dancers.

Her name on the show sign was Xena from Xanzibar. Her real name, she told me was Helen MacCoy. That turned out not to be true neither. But I didn't really care about her name. She was what they call a contortionist, which meant she could wrap her ankles around her neck and walk on her hands. She did that for me buck naked and she fucked me that way, which was surely the most exciting way I had done it in a while, if ever. And she loved to fuck while she was twisted up into all kind of other pretzel shapes, too. I never had met a woman who liked sex, any kind of sex, as much as she did.

I was so hot for her that I was ready to follow her anywhere, even to Tennessee when she told me that she had to leave the carnival for a few weeks to go there to see her brother about a family emergency. Her real name, she finally told me when we was on the road, was Bettie Jean Gates. We went to Cookville, Tennessee in the car I had stole from my cousin. It had a new paint job, lots of new parts, and Florida tags I had took off a Buick in Lake Wales.

What she didn't tell me, so I didn't know it at the time, was that I wasn't the only person who was hot for Bettie Jean Gates. The law in five states was looking for her ass. When we got to Cookville, we checked into a motel, and she took a carton of cigarettes and some money out of her suitcase and asked me to take them four blocks up the street to her brother who was in the Putnam County Jail. He needed the money for bail, she said.

That was when she explained why she couldn't go in, that she was wanted in Tennessee for forgery and larceny after trust, and in West Virginia for accessory to armed robbery, and in Kentucky for forgery and grand theft auto, and in Ohio for forgery and armed assault, rolling an old guy in a motel, and in Virginia for forgery, grand larceny, burglary and escape.

I had my own problems with the law and I damn sure didn't need to take on hers. If I'd been smart I would have parted ways with her right then and there, but she could read what I was thinking like it was a book page. Quick as a whip, she pulled off her dress and didn't have nothing on under it then she got on the bed and wrapped her ankles back of her head, rolled over and said, "everything's open, take your pick." When she contortioned herself like that, I got so crazy hard I would do anything she wanted.

I went in the Putnam County Jail and saw her brother. They didn't look at all alike, but I didn't think much about it. He had the same name as her, so I gave him the carton of Pall Malls and the envelope of money. When I walked back to the motel, my car was gone. I thought maybe she had took it to get us some burgers and beer for supper. I had left the keys on the dresser, and she had done her share of driving on the way up from Florida, so I didn't think her using the car was no big deal until I walked inside the room and saw that her bag and clothes was gone, too.

Then I began to worry and wonder, but I was too tired to do much thinking. We hadn't stopped nowhere to sleep on our trip just took kitty naps and spelled one another driving. I walked out and got an RC out of the vending machine and went back in the room to drink it, and smoke a cigarette, and start figuring what to do. Then I thought to myself, fuck her. Either she would come back or she wouldn't. My onliest inconvenience might be having to steal another car. In a few minutes I was asleep.

I was wrong again. Just before dawn the door busted open and my room was suddenly full of lawmen. They rousted me, cuffed me, dragged me to a car, threw me in back, took me straight to the county jail, hauled me upstairs, and put me in a holding cell. And all the time I didn't have on nothing but my under shorts.

That was one more pissed off bunch of lawmen. It seems that the carton of Pall Malls I had brought into the jail had a straight razor blade taped between the layers of packs of cigarettes, and just after midnight, Bettie Jean's brother, who it turned out was actually her husband, pulled the razor on the night guard and got the jail keys and escaped.

While I could appreciate the cleverness of their plan, I wasn't too happy with the notion that what they done was going to get me charged with aiding and abetting escape.

The law stripped off my underwear, searched my ass and mouth, and made me put on county jail coveralls, with wide black and white stripes, the uniform I would be wearing while I served my sentence on their chain gang.

When the sheriff interrogated me, I told him my name was David Gaskins, which was the name of my cousin whose car I had stole, and that I didn't have nothing to do with any escape, that I had met this here woman and shacked up with her and she asked me to do her a favor and deliver cigarettes and bail money to a man she said was her brother. I swore I didn't know there was a razor in the carton. Besides, I said, if I was in on their plan, would I have gone to sleep in a motel four blocks from county jail while they escaped in my car?

The sheriff allowed as how what I said made some sense. He got me to give him a description of my car and its license plate numbers to add to his all-points bulletin for the escapee and his wife. Then he asked me for some identification and I said the bitch had stole my wallet with my driver's license and all my other IDs. The sheriff was real understanding and said I could use the jail phone later to call somebody to send me some money and that he wasn't going to hold me. I was feeling as relieved as a newly unconstipated elephant.

He put me back into the holding cell and had some food sent to me and said I would be released as soon as he got the paperwork done. Seems to me the law always has two hours of paperwork to do for every one minute decision they make. A little later, a deputy came to my cell and said that my car had been found in the parking lot of the bus depot in a town thirty-five miles away. The sheriff had sent for it and they would let me know when it got there, then they would release me and my car and I could be on my way.

They gave me my clothes and my bag from the motel room. I was ready to go, but time dragged and I figured they was checking my car for clues to where Bettie Jean and her husband might've gone. I lay on the cot and smoked and felt calm as could be.

When the holding cell door opened and the sheriff and a deputy come in, I got up and smiled and started to put on my jacket and the sheriff knocked the shit out of me with a real round house punch. I fell to the floor with my nose and mouth bleeding like hell. He didn't like being lied to and made a fool of, the Sheriff said.

He had searched my car and in the glove compartment had found a tag registration in the name of David Gaskins, which is the name I had given him, but the certificate was for South Carolina license plates, not the Florida ones on the car. And the address on the registration said David Gaskins lived in Lake City, South Carolina, not Lake City, Florida, which is the address I had give him.

So he had called the law in Lake City, and they had said that David Gaskins did live there, and except for the color, the car sounded like the one which had been stole from David Gaskins a while back.

Then the Tennessee sheriff asked how could the car be a stolen car if David Gaskins owned it and drove it to Tennessee hisself?

That's when the Lake City lawman asked the sheriff to describe this David Gaskins that was in jail in Tennessee, because he had just had coffee with the David Gaskins he was talking about in Lake City, South Carolina not an hour before that. When the Sheriff described me, including the words Pee Wee tattooed on my shoulder, the Lake City lawman knew who I really was and told the sheriff that I was wanted for escape from the South Carolina Penitentiary where I was serving a sentence for assault and murder. The sheriff locked me up on a fugitive warrant then had me charged with helping Bettie Jean's husband to escape.

The Tennessee judge give me six months for that. And I caught three months more for cutting another prisoner. The way that come about was this. All the jail inmates had give me my due respect after the local newspaper wrote me up as a murderer escapee, except for this one asshole who said he didn't believe a little shit like me was a true power man. Soon as I got hold of a knife, I took off about half of his ear. That convinced him.

When my Tennessee time was up, South Carolina extradited me. Back at the state pen, I was put in the maximum security unit. I was still a power man, but in name only. I had my reputation, but if I was going to operate like I done before I escaped I needed to be part of the general population, running my scam in the shop, dealing during free time, keeping things straight for himself on the tiers and in the yard. In maximum security, I was in a one man cell from supper until breakfast and during the day I couldn't go out of the unit except for one hour in a fenced bullpen.

It was while I was locked down tight and bored shitless in MSU that I started doing more serious reading. I hadn't never got real good at it, not even in reform school. It was just too damn tedious. But the more I read, the easier it got and soon I found out there was all kinds of places and peoples and ideas I hadn't never heard about before. I guess books was the onliest things that kept me from going total crazy during all the years I was locked up.

I made it a point to try to be friendly with the guards, but because of my reputation they was real suspicious of me. When I asked if I could get a job working in the guard kitchen learning how to cook for the duty shifts they said, "hell no," but I kept on asking until finally I was put to work there part time. In just a little while, I was the second cook.

But I was still locked away in a solitary cell at night and restricted to the maximum security unit all the time. It was a miserable fucking life, and I knew I was going to have to serve out the rest of my sentence like that because the warden wasn't about to let me back into the general population where I could plan another escape. I didn't have hope for any charge so I tried to make the best of a real shit situation. Then, one of the greatest, importantest and luckies days of my life arrived.

I will always be grateful to, and owe a great debt to, The Federal Bureau of Investigation of Washington, D.C. for getting me out of maximum security then out of the whole damn South Carolina State Penitentiary, just at the time when I was feeling my downest. And the FBI not only rescued me, it also give me the opportunity to know some truly great men and get a truly fine education.

What happened was this. The federal law charged me with interstate auto theft for taking the car I stole in Lake City across state lines through Georgia, into Florida, and on to Tennessee. I was took from MSU to the Richland County Jail, Columbia, and kept there until I was tried in federal court and sentenced to three years in the Atlanta Federal Prison. On a motion from my lawyer, the federal judge ruled that my sentence would run concurrent with the time remaining on my South Carolina sentence and that on completion of my federal sentence, I was to be released without no liability for further time.

The Atlanta Federal Penitentiary was different. It was cleaner and moderner and stronger. It made the SC pen look like a cracker box. It had forty-foot high walls. The guard towers was manned twenty-four hours a day. Searchlights was on all night. The wall rule was, if you was in the yard and you touched the wall, the guard would fire a shot at your feet and if you didn't turn around and walk away from the wall the guard would shoot to kill you.

The prison was run by the rule book. Inmates stayed in line, did their work and spoke to guards only when they was spoke to. Visitor days was Saturday and Sunday, but I didn't have many visitors. My Mama had been able to get to Columbia from Florence to see me now and again, but her and the rest of my family didn't have the money or the time to come all the way to Atlanta.

In federal, the black inmates was mixed in with the whites, not separated like in the state pen. We all worked together and ate together and some even mingled in the yard and recreation rooms. We lived in eight man cells that was truly big. I mean with lots of room. Each inmate had his bunk and his locker. There was a commode and lavatory and shower in a separate little room next to the cell. And in the middle was a long metal table bolted to the floor with eight chairs so we could sit around and play cards and talk and visit. Nobody belonged to nobody. What inmates did was up to the inmates. There wasn't hardly ever any problems. Inmates didn't try to be tough and make their selves a reputation after they was inside. What you had been when you was outside, in the streets, determined your respect and your power inside.

The biggest power man in Atlanta Federal when I was there was Mister Frank Costello. He was in an eight man cell but with only two other men. They had been his lieutenants in the Genovese Family in New York and had come to prison with him on conspiracy charges. Almost every day, Mister Costello went to the prison hospital to be checked by the prison doctor and, some said, by his own personal doctor, because he was a very sick man. I never found out what with. Then he went to the prison library with his lieutenants. That was his assigned work, but I don't think he was actually made to do anything. He had lots of visitors. his lawyers came two or three times a week. They met in special conference rooms that had telephones and big chairs and tables reserved for meetings with lawyers.

I was in a cell with four New York men who had also been convicted with Mister Costello. There was two other men in the cell, both doing forty for bank robbery. Everybody in our cell was white. The New York men were special nice. They treated me like they had knowed me all my life. Second Sunday I was there, they took me to meet Mister Costello, who surprised the hell out of me by knowing so much about me, including why I had been sent to reform school. Soon as he shook my hand he said, "so you're the little hatchet man." And him and his men always called me that.

The first year I was in federal, I worked in CID, the clothing issue department, which was really the laundry supply room. I loaded up a big cart of uniforms and bed linens and pushed it around to the cells on two blocks.

Mister Costello didn't like prison issue sheets, and he didn't like sleeping on the same sheets two nights running, so first thing every morning I delivered his own special high quality sheets to his cell. I had to pretend I was sneaking them into his cell, and sneaking out his dirty sheets, because the guards weren't supposed to know what I was doing, or allow it to happen, but they really knew everything about it because it was arranged with them like all Mister Costello's privileges was.

The last two years I was there I worked in the prison industry making mail bags, which was kind of interesting and taught me a lot about leather. But my real education come during talks with my New York cellmates while we played cards in the cell or walked around in the yard. They were my professors.

Mostly they told me about how things was done in New York among men connected to one or another of The Families. Everything was based on silence, trust and loyalty. Omerta or Morte, they called it. Every man who worked with them had made his bones. They considered killing just a part of doing business.

The men in my cell were assigned to protect Mister Coste1lo. They had followed him to prison, and they had swore they would follow him to hell if need be. They told me that even though the Feds knew almost everything about Mister Costello and the rest of the Genovese Family, the only charge they could make stick was conspiracy because the things they did was kept separated so that nothing could ever be proved. Their sentence was five years, which they thought was a joke. They had been there six months when I arrived. They was released a year later.

The time I spent around them was my college education. Since then, every time I have been faced with a problem or a choice, I have thought back to things that they said to me and whenever I followed their advice I always came out okay. It was the times I didn't do what they advised that I found myself in deep shit.

They said that on the streets of New York, the toughest and smartest of their men were called wise guys. I called my cellmates The Three Wise Men. When they left, they each gave me a big hug, Italians do that a lot, and an address on Elizabeth Street in New York. They offered me a job when I got out. They said that a man like me could rise fast working with them, and since I had already made my bones, I was qualified.

Life in the Atlanta Federal Penitentiary got real quiet after they left there. I got an envelope from one of them two months later. In it was a paperback dictionary, English to Italian and Italian to English. And taped to pages inside was three one hundred dollar bills and a copy of that same address on Elizabeth Street, plus a telephone number.

I can't help wondering how different my life might've turned out if I had took them up on their offer and gone to New York and worked for them. As I already said, I will always appreciate the fact that I had the privilege of getting to know them men and learn from them. And I can truly say that I enjoyed the nearly three years I spent in Atlanta Federal Prison better than any other time I done inside. Never mind the rules was strict, nobody ever hassled me or give me any problems. I stayed straighter than I ever was before. I never got in trouble while I was there. I don't think I ever even got wrote up.

But don't get me wrong, I didn't have no desire to stay there permanently. I was real happy on August 6, 1961 when I got released, and was given a new suit and twenty dollars, and a bus ticket home to Florence, South Carolina.

The primariest problem outside on the streets was still the same, making a decent living. Because I had made some good money from time to time, I just wouldn't settle for less. There was jobs available in 1961, but the pay was less than what I made in Florida stripping and selling parts, and lots less than I made burning barns with Slick. At twenty-eight years old, there was just no way I was going to spend my life working for my Mama and stepdaddy on a tobacco farm in the Prospect community. I appreciated them taking me in when I first got out of federal and I did enough chores around their place to pull my weight while I was thinking on ways to make some real money.

Because I didn't want to upset my Mama, I tried hard not to let it bother me that my stepdaddy always acted like a dingle berried asshole. I was still littler than him so he bossed me around and talked real nasty to me like he had always done.

But then one day when we was working in the barn he made a real big mistake. He got mad about the way I was doing something or not doing something, I can't remember which, and he back handed me hard enough to knock me sprawling. I bounced up, mad as hell, and grabbed a pitchfork and backed him up against a stall. I was truly a cunt hair away from killing the son of a bitch but then I stopped. I couldn't kill him because, for some god knows what reason, my Mama loved that old sack of horseshit and I couldn't never do nothing to hurt my Mama, so I just pushed the prongs tight against his gut roll and told him how I made my bones in prison and that if he ever hit me again I would run him through in spite of my love for Mama.

The next day I decided that it was best that I moved out. I thought about getting on the road to look for the carnival and Poss, but that contortioned bitch had brought me nothing but grief and though the carnival was still a good place to hide out by blending in with drifters and roustabouts, it was a damn tough life moving every week with shit for pay.

I wasn't no escapee. I wasn't on the run. I could strip cars on my own, if that's what I decided to do. All I needed was to look clean and the law would probably leave me alone.

I stayed at my cousin Marvin Parrott's house for a while then I rented a little trailer on the farm where my Uncle Dewey lived. Marvin and Uncle Dewey was real nice about letting me use their cars. I did some job hunting and when I ran out of cash I did shade tree mechanic work. But I spent most all my nights hanging around honkytonks looking for something better.

My reputation had got to Florence and Sumter ahead of me. It was nice having men I had knowed all my life treat me with a kind off fearsome respect, hearing them tell other people who I was, then asking me, careful and polite, about the murder I did in prison, and about my escape. Though I never would explain how I broke out of the pen, I added to the stories by telling about my federal time that I done with Frank Costello who, the way I told it, had been my cellmate and become my close personal friend and had offered me a job in New York which I was thinking about going up there and taking. It weren't long before I made good connections for fencing stole property so I took up breaking and entering again, but I never did no local houses or stores. Most often I went to Columbia, or Charleston, or Charlotte in one or another borrowed car. Trouble was, I didn't know much about them cities or the neighborhoods and I was always afraid I might get surprised again like the time I was forced to defend myself when that girl attacked me with her hatchet. The next time it might be somebody with a pistol or shotgun.

Then I had another one of my lucky days. It was a Saturday and I was picking up a few dollars doing some mechanic work at a station near Leo when Reverend George E. Todd, who lived near my Mama and stepdaddy at Prospect, and who I had knowed a long time, brought in his vat type truck for a tune up.

We got to talking and he was real interested in my stories about prison life and working for the carnival, and when I told him I didn't have a regular job he said maybe I would like to work for him. He went all up and down the coast from north of Myrtle Beach to south of Charleston, sometimes even to Savannah, stopping at little towns and big towns, preaching and selling all kinds of things that store owners and just folks donated to his ministry so that whatever he made was all profit.

Now I want to make something real clear here. Preacher Todd was, and still is, a God fearing and honest man who supports his preaching with them donations of goods which he sold to keep going to the next preaching place. The fact that I worked for him don't in no way imply that he ever knew or had even the slightest idea that I was using him and his traveling and preaching as a cover for my breaking and entering.

During the first year that I worked for the Preacher, I rode in the van with him, he liked to do his own driving. By the second year , I had bought a station wagon and drove along behind him. Preacher Todd knew the coast of South Carolina better than any man I ever saw. We went to little back water places I hadn't never heard of and into knowed towns like Myrtle Beach, and Murrell's Inlet, and North Charleston, and Mount Pleasant, and Georgetown. He knowed folks everywhere and was knowed in return. Like the carnival, he had a schedule and was expected certain places on certain dates ever year.

Sometimes he preached revival at a church. Other times he preached evangelical outdoors under a canvas stretched between trees and the people brought their own folding chairs or pillows and blankets to set on. He always drawed good crowds. He preached hellfire and judgement with a voice that sounded like some kind of musical horn, powerful and mellow. I helped him set up and after the service I sold things for the Preacher out of the back of his van. He always explained to the congregations that the things he had for sale had been donated by other Christians so could be sold at truly bargain prices. And he asked that anybody who wanted to contribute any items to his ministry to bring them before we departed the next day. That's how the van always stayed full of merchandise. Things sold real fast and was replaced by even more, just as quick, at no cost. In Reverend Todd's words, he had a good, God blessed business.

As for me, I had my own blessed thing going, too. Because Rev. Todd was so respected, nobody suspicioned that when he was in town preaching, I was picking out good places to break into later. It didn't take me long to figure out that houses in beach towns was even easier pickings than ones out in the country. Folks near the beach and ocean tend to relax to the point of pure carelessness. I kept my eyes open for places that looked uppity rich and easy to get in, and a few weeks later, when we was preaching miles away, I slipped back and broke into them. I was real careful to check before I went in, to make sure no one was there.

And as we traveled around, sometimes I spotted and broke into country stores where I had seen racks of guns and displays of watches and such. Usually, I could haul away a thousand dollars worth in ten minutes. But I never sold out of the back of the Preacher's van any of the things that I had stole. I always fenced them things through two men in Sumter who I had knowed for a long time. They paid me real fair, about twenty cents on the dollar, so I had no complaints.

Driving along the coast behind Reverend Todd, I sometimes smiled to myself remembering the story of Jesus and the thief on the cross and I wondered how Christ would have felt having a power man for a partner. Of course I spent the biggest part of my time thinking about something lots more important than religion, pussy.

I didn't have no trouble picking up pieces of honkytonk ass around Sumter and Florence, but on the road it weren't so easy. We didn't usually stay anywheres long enough for me to get knowed, which, all things considered, I reckon was just as well, even though it meant that sometimes I wound up paying for a piece, which I didn't never like to have to do.

During 1962 I got married again. Her name was Jerrie Deloris and she was fine even though she was almost eighteen which was old by my standards. She was pretty, and nice, and sweet, and I treated her good, like I done all the women I married. She traveled with me some of the time and stayed with her folks other times. When we was apart, I telephoned to her when I could and sent her little presents and money. From then on whenever I was in a honkytonk where I didn't know anybody and a woman asked me to pay money for her ass, I said to hell with you, I got me a fine teenage wife waiting to fuck me when I get home.

Every six or eight weeks, Preacher Todd liked to go back to Prospect. He had his followers living around there, like my Mama, and he enjoyed being with his family. I enjoyed being with my new wife too, though I was usually restless to leave after a few days. It was almost the end of our second year working together that the preacher and the thief parted company. It weren't Reverend Todd's fault, it was my dick's.

I had knowed Patsy nearly all her life, which weren't all that long considering that she had just turned twelve when I statutory raped her. She stayed not too far away from my Mama's house and every time I went there to visit I seen her and got so hard I could hardly walk. I jacked a hell of a lot thinking about her and I bided my time. Then one Saturday when my wife had drove my station wagon to town to go shopping with her Mama, and I knew Patsy's folks was most likely gone too, I walked to her house and, sure enough, she was home alone.

She knowed me, of course, so she let me in when I knocked at the screen door and said I had just dropped by for a visit. I told her how pretty and growed up she was looking and other nice compliment things like that. Then I started talking about how many women I had fucked and how much they liked it, and I told her about the girl I had chopped with a hatchet, and the one I had beat with a hammer, and the man I had killed in prison. And all the while I was talking to her, I could see her getting scareder and scareder. Then she started crying, and I put my hand on her shoulder and steered her to the bedroom and said, "take off your clothes and lie down there and spread open your legs and I won't hurt you."

She done what I said and her body naked was more exciting than I ever could've imagined. Tiny tits and nipples, and a round little butt, and hardly no hair around her crack. That was the best piece of virgin ass I ever had, before or since, in my whole life. The onliest problem was that she got the sheets all bloody. Not just with cherry juice, but she started her ragtime, too.

While I was trying to figure how to get things cleaned up, I heard her two aunts drive up outside. I told Patsy we couldn't get caught naked. I made her get dressed quick, and we left the bloody sheets, and went out the back window, and ran cross country to my Mama's house and went to my room upstairs so I could have time to decide what to do. As it turned out, when her aunts seen them sheets, they guessed what had happened.

law men arrived at my Mama's house at almost the same time that her and my stepdaddy got home. From upstairs I heard a deputy say they had got a call from Patsy's aunt that she believed little Patsy had been raped and took off by Pee Wee Gaskins. The deputies said they was investigating the call and wanted to talk to me.

There was a big chifforobe in a corner of my room. I made Patty hide behind it and I was lying on the bed pretending I had been asleep when my stepdaddy and a deputy came upstairs. I said I hadn't seen Patsy, but my stepdaddy caught a glimpse her skirt poking out from behind the chifforobe and pointed to where she was. The deputy called his partner, and drew down on me, and made me roll on my stomach on the bed while he cuffed me. His partner dragged Patsy from her hiding place.

I was mad as a damn rattlesnake cornered in a corn crib. My own stepdaddy had turned me. Next time I got that bastard and a pitchfork in the same barn, I would shove the prongs plumb through his guts and out his asshole. They put me in the Florence County Jail and charged me with statutory rape, carnal knowledge of a twelve year old. They had the bed sheets sent to a lab. The blood was Patsy's, the semen was from a man with my blood type. My butt was in the sling again.

My lawyer said he would try to cut a deal with the prosecutor before my arraignment which was set for one week later at the Florence County courthouse. But during that week I give a lot of serious thought to how much I really didn't like the idea of going back to the South Carolina State Penitentiary, and I made some plans of my own.

When the county deputies transported me to the courthouse in the back of a patrol car, they handcuffed and manacled me, but once we was inside, in the defendant's waiting room on the second floor, they took off the cuffs and manacles and locked me inside the room to wait f23or my lawyer and the prosecutor to get there. Quick as a flea fuck, I jumped out the window.

It weren't barred. It weren't even shut. the law was damn sure nobody would be crazy enough to jump out a window thirty feet above the ground. But I was Little Pee Wee Gaskins who didn't weigh a hundred twenty pounds, shoes and all, so I just aimed my ass and back for the boxwood hedges that lined the sidewalk. All I got was some scratches and bruises, but I paid them no never mind. I was in a hurry to get out of them bushes and into one of them county cars parked next to the building.

    Like a few other times on other days in other places, I was lucky. I didn't even have to hot wire it, the key was in the ignition and I was miles out of Florence before anybody knew I was gone, much less commenced looking for me. I drove straight to Mama's house. She and my stepdaddy was gone to my arraignment. Mama always liked to support me by being in court whenever I was charged or tried or sentenced or anything like that. And my stepdaddy always liked to be there to give me his shit eating I told you so grin.

    I went upstairs and took my trucker's wallet of cash from where I kept it hid underneath the chifforobe, packed a zipper bag with clothes, and was gone again in less than five minutes.

    I knew that once the search started, it would be for that county car so I drove it out past Prospect and left it in a drainage ditch in three feet of water. Then I headed along back roads toward the town of Dillon. I didn't know that particular area real well, but I liked the way that the logging trails crisscrossed through the woods around swamps and back waters. That was the kind of place the Three Wise Men had talked about when they described New Jersey burying spots out of the way, with soft ground. I thought about them and smiled. I think I truly missed them.

    I made it into the edge of Dillon under dark cover and stole a 1962 Ford 500 Galaxy. Next day I was in Greensboro, North Carolina. I was on the run again, so I was looking for the carnival. According to my calculations, this was the time of year for them to be in that part of North Carolina, but in all the years that had passed their schedule had changed. The watchman at the fairgrounds said they had been gone two months or more and he wasn't sure where they were. I decided it wouldn't be too smart for me to drive a stole car all over the southeast looking for them.

That's when I remembered Poss telling me about Roberson County, the Lumbee Indian part of North Carolina, how you could get lost there and couldn't nobody find you and how them Indians didn't specially care much for the law because of the way they was treated so a wanted man could almost always find a safe place to hide out around there.

I had enough money to last me a while so I drove to a real small town and rented a room in a boarding house run by a Lumbee mama. I paid the rent for a month in advance and next day I drove the car all the way to Charlotte, and left it in a downtown garage, then took the bus to Raleigh and paid cash for an old car that barely got me back to the boarding house. With my landlady's permission, I parked the junker behind her house and proceeded to tear it down and rebuild it. I bought tools and parts, some new from a NAPA store, most from junkyards. Before long I had that '49 Ford singing to me.

Lots of evenings I went to one of the bigger towns in that area, usually to a picture show, then to a roadhouse, all of which sold beer, which was the onliest thing I ever drunk, and not much of that. Hard whiskey was illegal to sell by the drink, but there was moonshine for sale in hollering distance of all them places. But there weren't hardly ever no honkytonk women hanging around. Maybe a burned out old whore would show up some nights, but that was about it. Most of the men, Indian and white, came in with their own wives or girlfriends or they came in groups to drink and shoot bull. I didn't know how long I was going to be in those parts, but without a woman anytime would be too long.

At the end of my second month there I married a seventeen year old Lumbee girl named Leni. We met at the hardware store where she worked and I was mad hard for her from the first second that I seen her. We went out to dinner and to roadhouses and talked and laughed, but that was all she would let me do until I told her I loved her and wanted to marry her.

It never stops amazing me what a woman will do in exchange for them words. Not that I didn't mean it when I said I loved her and my other wives, too. I truly loved them all. Anyhow, we got married at her family's house and lived together for three months before I got so restless I couldn't tolerate it no more and one afternoon I told her I had to go buy some parts at the junkyard and I left the place where we lived, left Roberson County, and never had no intentions of ever seeing her again.

It weren't that I had stopped loving her, it was the weightiness and bothersomeness stirring around inside me. It seemed to be coming more often the older I got. And I didn't know how to deal with it in no other way except to just leave wherever I was and go someplace different. I got so edgy and mad at the world, I just had to get away.

I stopped in Charlotte and called one of my fences in Sumter and asked him if he knew where my wife Jerrie was. He said she was working in Johnsonville and living with some relatives of hers in Lake City. I called her at work. She was real careful and didn't let on to nobody that it was me. I told her to take a bus to Savannah, and get a room there, and go hang around the Crab's Tooth, which was a honkytonk we both knew with real good seafood, and I would meet her there one evening soon.

She said she would try, but I could tell she was pissed off at me. I guessed it was because I had fucked Patsy so I told her that I was sorry for hurting her, and wanted to make it up to her, and that if she would meet me we would go away together.

She showed up in Savannah two days after I got there. Together we headed for Florida. I tried to convince her that the whole thing with Patsy had been a setup deal, that her aunts just hated me. I don't know whether she believed me, our talking got interrupted when we arrived at Lake Wales and I was told the news about Poss. If you don't hear from or write to or talk with somebody for a few years their whole world can end and you don't know it because you've lost your links to them.

When I asked for Poss at the carnival office trailer the owner told me that almost two years ago Poss had got a call one morning that his new mobile home, a big long wide trailer off which the wheels had been took, had caught fire the night before—during one of them Florida freezes that nobody there ever seems prepared for. Poss's wife had bought a kerosene heater, and in the dark one of their littlest kids had got up, probably to go to the bathroom, and bumped the heater and knocked it over and the trailer caught fire. An open five gallon can of kerosene whooshed a fire ball from one end of the place to the other and between the smoke and the fire itself none of the family got out alive.

Poss had went home to a pile of ashes and the corpses of his wife and four kids and the next night he went to the funeral home and took a pistol from his pocket and lay down on top of his wife's sealed coffin and shot himself through the head.

After the carnival owner told me, I went outside the office and told Jerrie to go on back to the tourist cabins we was staying in, then I took a long walk alone. My head was filled up with the pictures of fire and the burned up bodies of Poss's wife and his little children who I had knowed and played with and I thought about Poss laying on that coffin with his head blowed off and I got real mad at him for killing hisself. I mean, what the fuck good did that do? It didn't bring nobody back. It didn't change jack shit. Then I decided I wasn't going to dwell on any of that no more, that that were the end of my knowing Poss. That was the all of it and that was that.

When I got to the tourist cabin, I was still feeling drag ass. I reckon I hadn't realized how much I was counting on seeing Poss and on hiding out with the carnival and going back to work stripping parts or finding something new and better to do. Now none of that weren't never going to be. The carnival owner who told me about Poss also told me that the girlie show operator had been arrested for running an interstate auto theft ring and was doing twenty in federal. He said everybody at the carnival had heard about me being arrested in

Tennessee from the lawmen who had come looking for Bettie Jean and her husband. Far as the owner knew, them two never had got caught. I thought to myself, if I ever catch up to that bitch I'll contort her into some shapes she ain't never been in before.

Jerrie and me left Florida the next day. She seemed even downer than me. She wanted to go back home. She said she didn't think things was ever going to work out between me and her. She didn't want to spend her life on the run with a wanted man. I had reached the point of uncaring a shit what she thought or done so I agreed to take her to Savannah so she could go back from there to Lake City and Johnsonville on the bus. I planned to head back to North Carolina, though just what I planned to do once I got there I didn't have a notion.

We crossed the Florida Georgia state line in late afternoon. I was thinking about Poss, remembering some good times. Jerrie was asleep and I guess was doing about seventy-five or more miles an hour when I heard the siren behind me and saw the flashing light. I knew that if I got stopped, I was going back to prison for sure so I floor boarded it, but that Georgia highway patrol car stayed right on my bumper.

Then my damned left front tire blew out, and I lost control, and went off the road doing maybe eighty-five or ninety. It was like what it must be like to fly a plane and to crash one. The only good thing was that the car come down on water, skimming along then stopping and starting to sink.

Swamps and me have been friends for all my years. I crawled out the window and stayed low in the saw grass and sloshed away from the road. At one point I turned and raised my head enough to see that there was now two patrol cars blinking their lights on the road, but I knew them patrol men weren't about to come in the swamp. They was most likely scared shitless of snakes, which made things just that much better for me.

I heard them yelling at Jerrie to raise her hands and walk toward them. I reckoned she was doing just that. I didn't wait to see. I kept sloshing away from them as fast as I could. I knew it wouldn't be long before more patrol men and lots of deputies arrived. And because of how stupid the law can get they would probably send for chain gangers and guards to go in the swamp after me with bloodhound dogs even though them dogs can't smell their own shit in water.

I made it to some dry ground by the time night got to be black dark. I could see car lights on the highway almost a half mile away. I walked parallel to the flow of lights, even when that meant getting back in the water for a few hundred yards. It weren't never deeper than my arm pits, and I was lots less worried about snakes than about some gun happy asshole shooting at me in the moonlight.

One thing about trying to get somewhere in the swamps, you don't ever get so tired you decide to lie down and sleep. I was still moving slow but moving, when the sun started up and all of a sudden another one of them pieces of pure luck kissed my dick.

I saw railroad tracks ahead of me. I knew that the highway that was a half mile or so off to my right was the one I had been driving on headed north. The sun was to my right. I was on course. The train tracks seemed to be coming from behind me, to my left, and heading off in front of me, bearing a little to the right toward what I figured was bound to be Savannah.

I found a patch of dry ground with high grass and scrub trees and cleared a spot and lay down. In the light, able to see what was around me, not just what I imagined might be there, I slept a little while. Thirst woke me up. That swamp water wasn't what you'd call fresh tasting, but at least it weren't brine. I felt rested and started walking again. The track bed was raised enough so I could see anything coming on the tracks or across the water. I walked all day and about dusk I come to a train yard on the edge of a small town. I never did know its name. I didn't go exploring to find out. Instead, I crawled into an empty freight car and went to sleep.

I felt the train pull out, heard it screech, and felt it slow down several times during the night. When it finally come to a dead stop and I looked out, we was in Savannah, Georgia. I had dried out but I wasn't much to look at. I made my way past some stock pens to a street where I found a run down hotel and got a room and took a shower. Later, I went out to a work clothes store and bought new overalls, underwear, shoes, and socks. I threw away everything I had been wearing and I headed for the bus station.

Two days and seven transfers later, I was back at the Lumbee Indian Lady's boarding house. She was real surprised to see me. The television and newspapers had run my picture and said I was an escaped killer who had died in a swamp in Georgia after wrecking my car while being chased by the highway patrol. I had been definitely identified as the vehicle's driver by my wife, Jerrie, who was with me but had been released from custody without charges.

My Lumbee landlady gave me a big hug and said she was glad I wasn't dead, though she didn't think my wife Leni was going to be thrilled to know I was alive and back to North Carolina, specially after seeing pictures of me and my other wife Jerrie on television.

I took my chances and went to see Leni. At first she didn't even want to talk to me, but gradually she started warming up when I told her my long story about me taking ill, and going to the veterans hospital in Oteen, and almost dying, and not having any identification on me and being sent to a special V.A. hospital in Augusta where they found my veteran's records and called my ex-wife Jerrie who come and got me and took me to her house in Lake Wales.

Leni seemed to believe me, but if my dick hadn't been so hard, I probably could have spotted the angriness smoldering inside her. But instead of noticing, I took her out to eat, then we went back to the boarding house and had us some long, easy love fucks and sucks, and I went off to sleep drained and happy.

Five lawmen woke me up. Leni had called them. When a woman decides to get her revenge, a man might as well bend over and kiss his asshole, dick, and balls goodbye. I got extradited and shipped back to the Florence County Jail and was there two weeks before the prosecutor and my attorney even bothered to come see me. I was cuffed, manacled, and guarded the whole two hours I talked with them. I didn't like the deal they wanted to cut for me so I turned it down. I was sure I could convince a jury that there was no harm and nothing wrong with me having sweet loving sex with a twelve year old girl, particularly when I hadn't physically forced her or threatened her or hurt her in any way. The jury didn't agree with me. The judge gave me six years for the statutory rape plus two more years for escaping from the Florence County Courthouse.

When I got to the South Carolina State Penitentiary this time, things was different. It was still the same dreary dungeon buildings, but it had a new name. The South Carolina Central Correctional Institution. CCI. The new Warden, Ellis MacDougald, had integrated black and white inmates in the same blocks, on the same tiers. We even ate together in the mess hall without no partitions. And now there was black guards. The warden called all this new shit a policy of rehabilitation not punishment. I was even give a list of inmate's rights along with the regular list of rules. And I heard that some inmates had gone so far as to file lawsuits against the warden and the Department of Corrections to get even more things changed.

I knew right away that the first and most important thing I had to do was find out just who the power men were and what was their thinking and advice on how I should deal with what was happening at this here CCI. Of course, I had already heard Warden MacDougald's Official Words. There weren't no power men any more. New policies no longer permit inmates to rule other inmates with force, terror and intimidation. Those days are gone forever from the South Carolina penal system. But wardens and administrators don't usually know baby shit from butterscotch pudding about what's going on inside. Only the inmates know truly what's what and what's not.

Finding the men who ran the inside didn't take long. The first day after I was processed, and evaluated, and let out in the yard, I met them. Fact is, they come to me. And right off they let me know that even if they weren't called power men, because that word upsets limp dick wardens, they still controlled things in the state pen, or CCI as it were now called. The onliest differences was that things were organized and done quieter so as not to attract no attention.

Blacks was in charge of blacks and the men with power all had nicknames. If you hadn't already earned a nickname outside in the streets, nobody called you by one inside. I smiled to myself. That was exactly what my cellmates in federal told me, what nick names meant in them New York Families like the Geneveses.

Suddenly things in CCI was looking better. If anybody wanted to know the prison's real pecker order, all they had to do was listen to the nicknames. The ones still called by their real names was all just meat.

That was 1964 and my nickname had come back to prison with me but Pee Wee didn't no longer have nothing to do with my size, you could bet your ass and your life on that. Every man who walked the yard or climbed a tier knew who I was, that I had made my bones and reputation inside CCI before there was a CCI, in the days when the old state pen was a fucking tough place.

My reputation started when I slit Brazell's throat, and it growed when I escaped, and it got bigger when the FBI snatched me out of MSU and sent me to do federal time alongside mister Frank Costello, biggest of the big New York Costellos, who had personally called me the Little Hatchet Man and offered me a job.

And my jumping out of the courthouse window and stealing the Sheriff's car, then escaping a manhunt after being reported dead in the Georgia swamps just helped my reputation even more. Now no one at the CCI dared to cross me.

Of course, Warden Ellis MacDougald said that power men didn't exist anymore and that he ran CCI, and today wardens still insist that they control the prisons, but all they really control are the gates, and walls, and fences that keep us in.

Anything we want brought in gets brought in. Anything. If there's any doubts at all about that statement, just keep reading my story to the end and you'll see. My final truth is the truth, theirs is the lie. It don't really matter what wardens, and lawyers, and judges, and prosecutors decide to call something, if it looks like an asshole and smells like an asshole, it's good for only two things, three, at most.

Telling about this sentence in CCI don't take many words. I'm really not evading or skipping over anything important. Nothing real important happened during them years. I did my time with hardly no problems to speak of. Prison life got even easier for me. I picked my own work, made my own routine, had anything I needed and mighty near everything I wanted.

Me and the other nicknames owned the yard and the inside. If I decided a piece of new meat would be nice, I had him sent to me. If somebody stepped out of line, my lines, I could get them set up and punished without worrying what would happen to me.

More and more I did things the way I had learned about from my cellmates in federal. I read and thought a lot about what the lawbooks said and from time to time I even called legal aid and they sent somebody out to visit me and discuss whatever I had on my mind. During those years I was real careful to keep my record clean.

Whenever I seen Warden MacDougald in the yard or the mess hall, I always said something friendly and polite to him. And if I got writ up, I went straight away and apologized to the warden and the guards, and then made sure somebody else's ass got blamed and put in the chopper.

Then, in the summer of 1968 I asked for and got an appointment with the warden in his office. I was ass pucker respectful and told him that I felt like his policy of rehabilitation not punishment had surely worked for me, that I had learned a lot, thanks to him, and since I had served more than four years without causing no problems, and had hardly even been writ up, I believed I deserved my full good time credits and I would truly appreciate him putting all of them in my folder along with a letter of recommendation to the parole board. That's how easy it was. There weren't nothing else to it. They paroled me in November.

8

The South Carolina Parole Board put a special condition on my release case. If I so much as set foot in Florence County for two years, I would be arrested and sent back to CCI. They did that, they said, because Florence County was where I had committed most of my crimes. Just how they figured the county line made a difference in what I did was beyond me, but that was their rule and I decided it would be best for me to abide by it.

I was thirty-five years old when I got out of CCI in '68 and I was damned determined I never was going back to prison, which didn't mean that I wasn't ever going to do anything illegal again, I just wasn't never planning on getting caught. To keep my record looking clean and straight, I went to live in the town of Sumter, in the county right next to Florence, and took a regular job for a construction company doing mostly roofing. But I did my real work and made my real money in the evenings and on weekends, stripping, reworking and repainting stole cars brought from out of state.

I rented a run down place quite a ways out in the country. The old man and woman who owned it was too feeble to farm anymore and was happy enough to get twenty-five dollars a month from me for an empty tenant house and barn half mile up a dirt track from where they lived. I used the tenant house mainly to store stole parts and the barn to do my car work. I fixed up both buildings so I could lock them tight when I weren't around.

I covered the windows and cracks so nobody could see inside, had the electricity turned on in the owner's name, repaired the pluming, and put a hot plate, and fridgerator, and table, and chairs, and a bed in the house so I could bring a stray piece there now and again, if she were a woman I'd as soon not take to my place in Sumter. It was a perfect setup for me then and suited my purposes even better later on.

Like I keep repeating, I had paid close attention to my cellmates from New York, and one of the importantest things I learned from them was how to stay two-steps away from doing any of the actual stealing or reselling. I was safe in the middle and always drove a good car and had more than enough cash in my pocket.

I was also doing some dealing in stole property that I bought cheap off a few of the teenage boys who worked construction with me and broke and entered in their spare time. Most of them used drugs, it was the big thing then, like it still is, and they needed money to support it.

Anytime I bought stuff from them, they could see that I carried a trucker's wallet full of cash, but I didn't never give no thought to me ever getting robbed until one Friday evening when I was buying some silverware in the parking lot back of a club and the two boys I was buying from, who was brothers, pulled knives on me and took all my money.

I was truly pissed off. I mean I got real mad. I had trusted them boys to deal fair with me like I done with them. Besides that, they knowed who I was, and what my reputation was, and still they robbed me. They needed teaching a lesson.

I went straight to the tenant house where I kept the onliest weapons that I owned. In the barn was a thirty-thirty rifle laying on a shelf in case anybody ever come snooping while I was working on a car, and in the house, in a zipper case under the mattress, was my Beretta automatic and a hand forged fighting knife called a Arkansas toothpick, with a leather fit handle and eleven inches of blade, double edged like what they call a stiletto, and honed straight razor sharp. It was purely the biggest and meanest looking knife I ever saw. I figured anybody with any sense at all would turn tail so I doubted I would even need to use it but if I did it would flat do the job it were made for.

I put the zipper case in my car and drove back to Sumter. I parked a block from where them two boys lived and I was waiting when they parked their pickup and got out. Because there was two of them, I decided to use the Beretta. I pointed it at them and made them get in the trunk of my car. I drove them twenty miles to a place in back water woods and I made them get out and give me all the money they had plus their watches and reefer.

Then I made them take off their clothes and I told them that if they ever crossed me again, I would string them up and cut off their halls. Then I left them in out the woods buck ass naked.

After that there was a more respectful and better attitude toward me amongst all the boys I bought from. But just to make damn sure that nobody ever robbed me again, from then on I always carried my weapons under the front seat of whatever car I drove.

All my family still lived in Florence County including my first wife, my only legal divorced ex-wife, and my little girl, who was about seventeen by then and married with kids of her own, as well as my Mama and her kin. We was close enough to one another to allow us to get together right often even though I weren't ever supposed to go into Florence County.

I stayed in different places in and around Sumter, with one or more women, usually in nice trailers. Of course, by then they was called mobile homes, which I remembered was what Poss's wife had called their trailer after she had the wheels took off.

I recollect how mad she got when Poss said it was still a trailer and she said, no, it ain't a trailer, it's a mobile home, and he said, how the fuck can it be a mobile home when it can't go no where because it ain't got no wheels. I wished old Poss could've seen me then, living in a mobile home, out of prison, near my family and wives and making damn good money.

Whenever I felt the need of a new piece of ass, strange stuff it was called then, there was always plenty to be found hanging around the honkytonks. Women had got lots freer with their pussy than I had remembered them being. I heard it was because of that new pill that made them not have to be afraid of getting knocked up every time they fucked.

In prison I had had to settle most of the time for just meat so I was of a mind to try a sniff and taste and feel of every woman I met. My favoritest kind were still honkytonk women, except that now lots of the tonks was called clubs. That was just another one of the things I had to adjust to being different from what they had been before '64 when I was sent off to prison. But I reckoned most of the changes that had took place was for the better and it seemed I had all the makings of a good life ahead of me.

But it didn't make no difference how agreeable and enjoyable things was, every once in a while my insides started getting them aggravated and bothersome feelings again. The same as I had got regular from time to time as long as I could remember. First that special heaviness commenced to roll around in my gut then up my spine and into my head and down again. I hurt from my balls to behind my eyes. It was a truly terrible kind of pain that felt like it wanted to tear me open so it could get out.

It didn't seem to be brought on by anything or anybody in particular, but when it come, I sure knew it was there. I got edgy, and upset, and mean as a cotton mouth moccasin in a gallon size mason jar. When I was like that, I knew the best thing for me to do was get far away from any folks that mattered to me. I sure didn't ever want to hurt a wife or kid when I exploded.

I would dive alone along the Carolina coast, on roads I had learned in '61 when me and the preacher made our trips. And whenever I saw a girl hitch hiking, which they had started doing a lot of around the beaches in the late

1960's, I would stop and give her a lift. I always asked where she was from and after we had rode and talked a few minutes I asked if she had a place to stay and offered to get us a motel room for the night. If she said no, then I offered her money for a piece of her ass or a blow job. If she said no again or got upset, I stopped the car real quick and let her out. I didn't want no trouble and I knew that if a girl got scared she could call the law, and I could be looking at six to ten just on her word, whether I did anything to her or not.

But even when I found one who needed money and serviced me, it never was exciting worth a damn to pay for what I could get free from a dozen women in Sumter, or Johnsonville, or Lake City.

After a while I started to wonder why the hell I was doing what I was doing? I damn sure wasn't hurting for another piece of ass. And when I was trying to figure it out I suddenly realized that the ones who stayed on my mind and upsetted me the most were them ones who had said no and got out of the car, like they was too damn good for the likes of me, like they was so special their shit didn't stink.

Them was the ones I truly wanted and I don't mean I wanted them just to fuck. I jacked a lot thinking about stringing them kind up by their heels and whipping them bloody, or doing some things lots worse, though I knew I couldn't really do nothing like what I was thinking without ending up back in prison.

Usually twenty-four hours of wandering up and down the coast made things inside me tolerable again. Whether I got any pussy or not, when the pain finally eased up, I pushed away what was left of aggravation and weighty feelings and drove back home. But after another few weeks, the bothersomeness always come back, and I had to take another drive to get away. It was like I was looking for something special on them coastal highways, only I didn't know what.

That's how it went that whole next spring and summer. Then one Sunday morning in 1969, when the pain was like plumbum in my bowels, and the weight was so heavy I couldn't hardly breathe, I left Sumter before sunrise and drove to Myrtle Beach. It was on that trip that a pure miracle happened and changed my whole life, as sure as Paul's was changed on the road to wherever it was he was going when that beam of light come down and brought him his miracle.

It was September. The beaches at Tybee, Folly, Pawleys, and Myrtle was mostly deserted after Labor Day. There weren't many girls on the roads, I doubt I had seen half a dozen all that day, and none alone. Back in the beginning, I didn't pick up twos and threes. It was midafternoon when I finally saw one hitching near the intersection of the road that comes over the causeway from Pawleys Island. She was blonde, tanned, and better looking than most. I figured her for maybe eighteen or nineteen, old enough so there wouldn't be any of that statutory shit if she said yes. I stopped. She got in and put her duffel bag on the back seat. I asked where she was going. She said, Charleston tonight, Jacksonville tomorrow. She was meeting friends and they were going to Miami to work on a yacht. I said that sure sounded exciting.

Then she started talking a mile a minute, not hardly stopping to breathe, telling one story after another about working on a yacht the year before, sailing to all them Caribbean island down south of Florida. First chance I got, I interrupted and told her I hadn't actually planned to drive no farther than Georgetown that afternoon but I would gladly take her all the way up to Charleston where we could have supper at a nice restaurant and share a hotel room.

She laughed one of them kind of nervous bust out loud laughs, but it didn't make me mad. Fact is, I don't recall feeling anything much when she did it. I just kept my eyes on the road and stayed calm and said yes or no?

She said no thanks and laughed that same laugh again. And I said well whatever you want is fine with me, but you'll have to get to Charleston on your own because I don't do nothing for nothing in return. And she said okay, you

88

can let me out here.

In those days the stretch of highway south from Myrtle Beach to Georgetown was two lane blacktop, narrow with no shoulders, and drainage ditches on both sides. It was a couple of miles before I got to a dirt road where I could pull off. When I stopped, I turned sideways on the seat and stared at her and that was the moment when my miracle come shining down. Now don't get me wrong, I know I didn't see no real beam of light like Paul said he saw, but I did find my answer surely as he found his. And the answer was simple. What I had to do was kill her.

I remember smiling to myself and wondering why I hadn't ever thought of that before? If she was dead, she couldn't never tell the law or nobody nothing so once I had made up my mind and decided that she was going to die anyhow, I could do anything I wanted with her.

Anything.

I kept smiling and draped my arm over the seat and waited. She smiled back at me and turned to reach for her duffel bag. I slammed my fist into the side of her head and knocked her against the dash. I hit her twice more and she fell to the floorboard.

She didn't move. I took off her belt and used it to tie her hands behind her back. I took off my belt and looped it around her neck. Then I looked at her again and remembered something one of the Three Wise Men from Elizabeth Street once said. Killers don't get caught if bodies don't get found.

I drove down the dirt road a quarter mile to where it dead ended at what had been a logger's turn around where they dragged felled trees and sawed them to load on the flatbeds. There was a sawdust mound and a rusted pulley and hoist chain.

She was getting over being stunned, and I could see she was trying to figure what was happening and what she ought to do. I opened the car door, grabbed the end of the neck belt, and pulled her out the driver's side and she landed on the ground on her back.

Every time she yelled, I jerked the belt and she choked and sputtered. But she kept on yelling and trying to get up until finally I reached under the car seat and pulled out my zipper case and took out the Arkansas toothpick. I put the tip of the blade barely inside the nostril of her nose and told her to shut the fuck up. She got real quiet real quick. Then I ripped off her shirt. She wasn't wearing no bra. She had little tits, which I guess went with her being tall and skinny. Then I took off her sandals and jeans, then her panties, and spread her legs wide apart. She was a real blonde, but she didn't have much hair. Maybe she shaved around it. I didn't ask. All I could think about was that I could do anything I wanted to her. I opened the car trunk and threw her clothes inside.

Then I undressed and made her suck me. A minute or two was all I wanted. I could get a blowjob anytime, this was going to be something special. I pushed her onto her back and I straddled her stomach and said polite as you please, "do you mind if I suck your tittie?"

She looked at me kind of funny and said, "okay."

So I pinched her nipple tight between my left thumb and finger and pulled it away from her chest as hard and far as I could and sliced off about an inch of her tit with the nipple. She screamed. I pulled the belt and choked her quiet. Then I held the nipple between my front teeth and smiled. Blood from it dripped on her face. She was sobbing like a baby.

I said, "don't cry, I'll share it," and I put the nipple between her lips and told her to suck it. When she did, I shoved the whole slice in her mouth and made her chew it up and swallow it. She gagged and tried to get up, then she vomited all over herself and me, which truly pissed me off because there just weren't no call for that.

I stood up and stomped her pussy bone hard as I could and wished I hadn't already took my heeled boots off. Then I knelt down and turned her on her stomach and started fucking her ass. She kept on crying, "it hurts, please stop."

So I tightened the belt around her neck to make it hurt even more. And after I corned, I made her lick me clean.

By then it was late afternoon, and I knew I had best move fast. I decided to wait and kill her where I buried her, like they had told me was the best way. I sure didn't want to spend hours cleaning my car. Blood is damn hard to shampoo out of upholstery. I tied her shirt around her chest, to soak up the blood from her sliced off tittie.

She had trouble trying to stand up. She kept moaning and crying. I put the knife on the car seat and picked her up gentle and laid her inside the car trunk. I told her that if she kept quiet and didn't give me no trouble, I would let her live. She said, "thank you."

I once read in a book about the Nazi death camps that the best way to get somebody to cooperate when you plan on killing them is to promise them that if they do what you tell them to do, they won't die. And you can take my word for it, it works.

I closed her up in the trunk, got dressed, walked to the shack, picked up the rusted pulley and chain, and put them in the car. South of Georgetown I stopped at a country store gas station and spoke just loud enough for her to hear me and told her I was buying gas and for her to please stay quiet. There wasn't a sound from the trunk while I put in three dollars worth of high test and went in the store to buy a fifty foot length of clothesline.

Then I drove a little farther down the coast to where the marshes come close to the highway and they're thick with saw grasses and swamp plants. Marsh bottom is like quick sand. Anything weighted sinks deep and there are crawlers, not big but lots of them, that will come to blood and eat most everything and turn it into crawler shit. When I spotted a turn-off, I drove onto it real slow for about two hundred yards to a dump point with marsh on three sides.

I pulled her out of the trunk, rolled her on her stomach, took my belt off her wrists and tied them with a piece of clothes line. Then I stuffed her panties in her mouth and cut off part of her shirt and gagged her with it. She was having trouble breathing, but that didn't matter much any more. She knew I wasn't tying her up to rape her again.

I watched her watching me. She whined. Her eyes was pleading with me not to kill her. I said, "beg, bitch," then I left her laying on the ground while I walked back along the trail until I found a tree limb about six feet long and dragged it to the edge of the water.

She was laying on her side. I tied her knees together and looped the rope around her neck and drew her knees up to her chin. I made two more turns around her neck, tightened the rope and knotted it. She was doubled over, trussed for butchering, her head and legs on one end, her cunt and ass on the other. Her eyes bulged. I slid the point of the knife a full inch into her ass. Her eyes got even wider, like she knew what was coming.

Then, real slow, I pushed all eleven inches of toothpick blade inside her, all the way up to the hilt, and I sliced upward as I pulled it out. Where she had two little holes now she had one big one. She twisted and jerked, trying to scream. I wanted real bad to take of her gag so I could hear her, but I would've had to be crazy to do that.

Always weigh bodies down heavy.

I remembered what they said and roped the logging chain and pully around her. Then l dragged her to the water, draped her across the pine limb and floated it out as far as I could reach and dumped her off. I watched until she had sunk so deep there weren't no trace of her. She didn't make bubbles for very long.

I went to the car and put her duffel bag in the trunk with her clothes. That was when I noticed the wallet in her jeans. Inside it was a twenty dollar bill and six ones. I had been so caught up in what I was doing I hadn't thought about her stuff. I dumped everything out and went through it.

What that girl was doing hitching was a mystery. She had three hundred dollars cash in a pocket book inside her duffel. There was identification, too. Best as I can remember, her name was Leela or Lila something from some state up north, seems it was Massachusetts, but I'm not sure. That was a lot of years ago and a lot of bodies ago and frankly I didn't give a flying fuck who she was, or where she come from.

To me, everything in her duffel was just evidence like her body was and I didn't want any evidence ever to connect her to me, so I didn't keep nothing but the cash and a few things I knowed couldn't be traced.

I stuffed everything else back in the duffel, added a few rocks, tied it closed, and threw it as far out in the marsh as I could. For a minute or two it looked like it was going to float, but then it started down. When it finally went under, there weren't anything to see but grass and water.

It was dark and raining by the time I got to the truck stop cafe half way to Sumter. I was so damn hungry I ate the biggest steak on the menu and I left the waitress a five dollar tip. Driving the rest of the way home that night I played the radio real loud and sang along with it. I felt truly the best I ever remembered feeling in my whole life.

All the bothersomeness inside me had sank into the marsh with that girl. And from then on, whenever the pain came back, I knowed what to do to get rid of it.

9

Next morning I woke up sweating and shaking. I had even wet the bed which was something I hadn't done in a real long time. I was so awful upset because I knew I had did something bad wrong. I had committed a murder without any proper planning and preparing.

I vowed I wouldn't never make that mistake again. Never mind that I remembered to follow most of the advice give me by my three wise friends. If I hadn't been just plain lucky things might have turned out terrible. What if I hadn't brought my toothpick? What if that girl had got loose and out run me to the highway and a car had stopped for her? Or what if she hadn't stayed quiet at the gas station and started screaming and the store owner called the law? Even if I had drove off, he probably could've identified me and my car.

Stopping at that store to buy clothesline was one of the stupidest things I ever done. I had to make real sure I never did anything like that again. From now on, whatever I needed I ought to carry with me. I started buying stuff to put in a duffel bag I could always carry in whatever car I drove, like I did my zipper case and rifle.

I never bought much at any one place. Most things I got one at a time in places where nobody likely knowed me. At pawn shops in Columbia, I bought handcuffs. In other towns I bought chains and rope and duct tape. It got to be kind of a hobby, looking around whenever I was in a hardware store, figuring how I might use tools and other stuff in ways different from what they was made for. I added things like hoses and a hand pump, a blow torch, acids, lighters, hammers, hatchets, awls, and cables.

There never was no doubt in my mind that I was going to do it again. Grant you, I dwelled on it some because I knew the law held murder seriouser than rape or burgling or car stripping, but I figured it was worth the risk to rid myself of them spells of pain that had plagued me all my life. My only concerns was being prepared. I planned ahead real careful, so as not to leave things ever again to be done on the spurs of moments.

Some Saturdays and Sundays I drove along the coast, not looking for hitch hikers, just searching out places. On back waters of the Pee Dee River, near where I had worked with the cypress cutting and hauling crews, I found old logging roads that went for miles into the swamps and more trails into marshes south of Georgetown, and nearer Charleston and Bluffton and Beaufort. There was so many good places, it was hard choosing.

I decided on spots I could get to quick from main highways, but far enough away so I wouldn't have to worry about anybody seeing or hearing, and I always picked spots that had a nice burying place close by. About six weeks after I done that first girl the bothersomeness come back and I went looking for another one. Once I found her, things was a whole lot easier because now I had everything clear in my mind.

I took my time and did some of the extra things I had thought up so I enjoyed myself more and after I finished I felt that same good relief I had felt the first time. By Christmas of 1969 I had done the first three of what I called in my mind coastal kills, ones where I didn't know the victims or their names or nothing about them except that they was what I had went looking for and found. The reason there was only three that year was because I didn't get started until September. During 1970 there was more. One about every six weeks or so, on average.

There weren't nothing out of the ordinary to tell about most of them. It was my first full year of that sort of killing and for the most part I was setting up my methods that never changed much. When I picked up one and we rode aways, I drove off the highway onto a trail and before she could say anything I pulled my pistol and told her to do what I said.

I truly hoped I never had to use that Beretta. I didn't want to get blood and bone and shit splattered all over the inside of my car. After I handcuffed her, I drove to a spot I had already picked, and we got out and I stripped her and did whatever I wanted.

Some of them I cut. Some I burned. I ran a cable in and out one and hung her up by it. I pumped another one full of water, which seemed to really hurt, filling her up until it came out her nose and mouth, but she died quick, which I hadn't expected, so I didn't do that anymore. I preferred for them to last as long as possible.

I took my time, and when I finished, I usually killed them the same way I did the first one, weighting them down and drowning them, taking care of killing and burying both at the same time. First, though, I always took off the cuffs and tied their wrists with rope. It seemed crazy to sink expensive handcuffs like that.

By October of '70, I had picked up and coastal killed ten girls total including the three done in '69. But the most important thing about 1970 was that it was the year I started doing my serious murders.

I admit that from time to time I had got mad at people who I knew and I even inflicted a little grave bodily harm on some of them, like what I done that got me sent to reform school, and to prison the first time. But I swear that up until 1970 I hadn't never give any real serious thought whatsoever to killing anybody that I ever knowed personally. And before I go any further with this part of my story, I need to tell a little about Sumter, South Carolina.

It's not a big town. Everybody pretty much knows who everybody else is though there is layers of folks that don't have nothing to do with those living on different layers, like I reckon things is most everywhere. For the most part, people speak to one another and is friendly and polite.

Whenever I saw women and girls I knew in clubs, or at the drive-in restaurant, or in a store, I stopped and talked to them. Most times it was just idle chatterings, but sometimes some of them seemed interested and we made a date, and later we went to my place, or parked somewhere for a little love fuck.

Still and all, like I already said, I hadn't never thought about coastal killing any of them girls that I knew. I guess the reason for that was because I had always left Sumter and gone to the coast when the bothersomeness come, so I never mixed the two in my head. Howsomever, in November of 1970 that changed.

Most weekends I stopped by the drive-in for a burger and saw my sister's daughter, Janice, who was fifteen, with a bunch of other girls and they always flagged me down and asked me to buy beer for them, which I wouldn't do, not because it was against the law but because I really didn't like seeing kids who was that young drinking alcohol.

Though I didn't approve, I did kind of like having them ask. After while it come to be a joke between us, they teased me about being too religious to buy beer. I teased them back saying I'll buy you a six-pack when you're old enough to party with me. Mainly I egged 'em on just for the pleasure of being close to that much young stuff. I got along special well with Janice. I had stayed at my sister's house time and again when I was between mobile and between women and Janice and her friends all called me Uncle Pee Wee. So I wasn't really too surprised one night when a carload of girls I recognized drove up beside my car and waved me to stop. I pulled over and they parked beside me.

One of the girls got out and said that Janice had drunk some beers and couldn't go home until she was sober, which might take a while, but the girl whose car they was in had to be home by ten and it was already five after so could her and Janice get in my car until Janice got straight, then I could take them both home, would I do that, Uncle Pee Wee, please?

Of course I knew the girl. Her name was Patricia Ann Alsbrook. She was a couple of years older than Janice. They was friends and run around together. I said, okay sure, I would do what she asked. So she went back to the other car, and her and Janice walked to my car, and both got in the back seat. Then the other car left and I drove to the drive-in restaurant and ordered us some coffee.

Janice took a couple of sips and vomited all over the back seat, which upsetted Patricia Ann more than it did me. She apologized and said she would clean it up. Then I took a long look at them two girls, and I got a different idea. I said I thought Janice needed a cold shower and she could take one at my house. When Patricia Ann agreed, I knew she thought I meant at the mobile home where I lived in Sumter. She was too busy holding Janice's head while Janice puked to notice when we drove out of Sumter.

finally, she looked out the window and said where are we going? And I said we was going to my place in the country. Patricia hesitated a little when I stopped in front of that ramshackle tenant house, but she didn't say nothing else, she just helped me get Janice inside into the bathroom that had a pipe stemmed shower over the tub.

I turned on the water and started unbuttoning Janice's blouse and Patricia Ann said, "let me do that," and I smiled and said, I'm her uncle, I been bathing her all her life. Patricia Ann shrugged and we both finished taking off Janice's clothes and holding her under the shower. Of course, me and Patricia Ann both got completely soaked too and in a few minutes we was all laughing a lot.

I turned off the water and got a towel and started drying Janice who giggled and said she had to pee. Patricia Ann helped her to the toilet. I said, "when she's done you all come in the bedroom. I've got some spare dry clothes. They won't fit too good but they'll do." By then I knew that even though Patricia Ann was embarrassed, she had pretty much decided everything was okay, including Janice being naked, and me helping them and all.

By the time her and Janice got to the bedroom, I had got my zipper case from the car and was waiting. I complained about being wet and took off my boots and shirt. Patricia Ann helped Janice lie down on the bed and put a sheet over her. Then I took off my pants and shorts and let Patricia Ann see the state I was in. One look and she started toward the door, but then I drew the toothpick and pointed it at her and told her to sit on the bed. She started to say something, but I told her to just be still and I wouldn't hurt her. I just aimed to teach Janice not to ever get so drunk again. Patricia Ann sat quiet while I turned Janice on her back and propped her legs open and took a close look and quick taste, then laid on top of her.

Janice sobered real quick and commenced to fight me, but the toothpick blade pressed against her neck settled her down. Then, just as I was set to slide in and pop her cherry, something hit me on the back of the head like a mule kick. Everything went silver, then black.

It was probably a minute or three before I come to and shook out the dizziness. I looked to see what it was that hit me, but only seen that both girls was gone. I pulled on my pants, grabbed my pistol and a flashlight, and went after them. They was running on the dirt road toward the highway. I jumped in the car and chased them. When I got close, they ran into the woods. I got out, and fired a shot in the air, and yelled stop, and they stopped.

I didn't take no chances. I opened the car trunk and made them get inside. Once we was back at the house, I got my duffel bag out of the truck when I let them out and we went to the bedroom. I shoved them both towards the bed and told Patricia Ann to take off her clothes.

She said, "no," so I back handed her across the face with the pistol barrel. Her glasses went flying across the room and blood come pouring out of her nose. She fell onto the bed, holding her face and crying. I told her to shut the fuck up and take off her clothes or I was going to shoot her. And while I was putting all my attention into watching her get undressed, damned if Janice didn't jump up and run for the door. I caught her just as she flunged it open. I grabbed the pistol by the barrel and smacked her on the side of her head with the butt. She dropped to the floor.

And when I turned back around, damned if Patricia Ann weren't headed toward me with a piece of two-by-four which I guess is what she had hit me with before and was aiming to hit me with again.

This time I jumped out of the way when she swung it at me, and I grabbed her hair and put the pistol against her nose that was still bleeding, made her drop the two-by and marched her back to the bed, and shoved her on it, on her stomach, and handcuffed her. Then I went back and handcuffed Janice who wasn't breathing too good. Every few seconds her body jerked and twitched like she was having some kind of convulsion spasms. I put the pistol down on the floor and picked her up and carried her to the bed.

Then I recommenced stripping off Patricia Ann's clothes and even though she was handcuffed, damned if she didn't fight me like crazy, kicking and bucking and struggling to get up. There was just no way I could hold her down and at the same time keep an eye on Janice who I couldn't be sure wasn't possuming and getting ready to jump up and run again and I knew right then and there that them two was more than I could handle and they didn't really leave me no choice in the matter. I had to kill them both.

When I think back on it, I'm sure the coastal killings that I had did made it a whole lot easier for me to decide Janice and Patricia Ann had to die. Killing girls weren't no longer new for me. I had learned how to do it proper and right and once I set my mind to kill there weren't no changing it. Of course, this time there was one difference. I hadn't never had no kind of connections with any of them coastal kills, but I was damn sure connected to Patricia Ann and kin to Janice and there was bound to be questions asked of me when them two didn't never ever come home again.

I decided it would be better to think about that problem later. Right then I had to stop Patricia Ann's fighting with me so I picked up the pistol and hit her square on the top of her head.

Now I had two naked teenage girls on my hands, and they was both unconscious so I needed to figure what to do next. Killers don't get caught if bodies don't get found. I thought about the marshes, but the coast was too far away. I had to bury them close by, but where nobody would think to search for them. Then quick as a snake strike the answers come and I knowed exactly what to do.

I looked at my watch. It was barely midnight. Janice was already almost dead. And I couldn't get hardly no reactions at all from Patricia Ann no matter what I done. Her friends called her Patty, but I wasn't never her friend.

So I give up messing with them and searched the car and house for their purses and clothes and I redressed them, not because I thought they needed dressing for killing and burying, but because I knew that was the best way to make sure I had found everything they had brought with them. I didn't want no evidence laying around the house or car.

I left Janice on the bed and carried Patricia Ann to the car trunk. I took my zipper case with me, along with one thing from the duffel, a ball peen hammer. I drove to a house that I knew was vacant and had a big septic tank. I toted Patricia Ann from the car to the tank and put her down. It took all my strength and straining to move the cement slab cover off the tank.

I planned to crack her skull open to make sure she was dead, but I decided that would make too big a mess, so I just lowered her into the sludge and waited until there wasn't any more bubbles, then I pushed the cement lid back in place.

When I got back to the tenant house, Janice was definitely dead. I carried her out behind the barn and dug a grave. The ground was loam, easy to shovel, but still it took me the best part of an hour to get it deep enough to where she wouldn't get dug up by animals. I smoothed the ground and next day I brought a load of pine needles and scattered them to cover the fresh dug earth. I buried their purses near The Neck.

Like I expected, there was lots of questions asked me for a long time because Janice and Patty's friends all told everybody including the law that the last time they seen Janice and Patty, they was both with me. I admitted to the girls's families including to my sister, who was Janice's mama, and to lawmen, that the girls had got in my car and we had gone to the drive-in. I said that while we was there Janice had asked me about some of our kin people who lived in California and that her and Patty both said they was unhappy in Sumter and was thinking about running away.

Then, I said, the two girls got out of my car and into a car with some boys they knew, who I believed they said was from Orangeburg, and I left them there and I never seen them after that. The families and all their friends stayed upset about Patty and Janice being missing, but the law soon got busy with more important things and acted like them two girls was nothing more than just another couple of runaways.

The law didn't find Patricia Ann Alsbrook's body until six years later, in 1976, and even then it weren't no piece of brilliant police work. They found her only because I had ended up on Death Row, looking at The Chair for the first time, and I weren't fond of the idea so I did a tip about Patty's body in the septic tank to prove I knew things that might could become part of a deal.

To show just how retarded lawmen can be, eight years after Janice disappeared, and two years after they was told where Patricia Ann was buried and had dug her up and identified her, they still hadn't found Janice's body. Some dumb ass spokesman for the law was even quoted saying that since she wasn't buried with Patty that meant she probably had run away somewhere all by herself.

That was in '78 when I made my deal to beat The Chair the second time by showing them more graves. Since they had already dug up Patricia Ann, the prosecutor wanted Janice's body too, as part of the deal. I couldn't refuse because when we was negotiating I had admitted killing both girls.

But I had a problem. Near where I buried Janice, I later on had buried some others that the law didn't know anything about and still don't. The point is, them others weren't part of the plea bargain deal, and if I led lawmen to Janice's grave they would surely find them others and that would start a whole new investigation that could break my deal because I had swore on a polygraph and under truth serum that I had told them about all my kllings and if the law found out that weren't true, that there was more, it would fuck up my plea bargain and I needed to not fuck that up because it was my only chance to stay out of The Chair. So, to solve that problem, what I did in '78 was lead the law to the grave of a girl that I had picked up hitching near Columbia in 1973. She was about Janice's age and size, and I had buried her near Prospect.

When l showed the law where to dig and they found the body, some of them SLED Agents questioned why I had buried Patricia Ann in a septic tank outside Sumter then drove all the way to Prospect to bury Janice? I said it was because Janice was family and I thought she ought to be buried near our old home place. And, of course, the dick brains bought that one, too.

There was lots of family questions then, and there still are, about whether or not that was Janice's body. There was autopsy notes about x-rays of healed bone fractures that didn't jibe up and there was stories about dental records getting misplaced and mixed up during those eight years they was looking for her and sending charts all over the country for comparing with unidentified bodies.

To complicate things even more, some of my family come to see me in prison in '79 and asked me if that body was really Janice. I said "no, it was not." Then I told my kinfolks that I was forced to say it was Janice to satisfy the prosecutor by providing a body in order to stay out of The Chair.

I swore to them I never killed Janice, that me and Patty put her on a bus for California then Patty got high on drugs and her and me argued about having sex and I killed Patty,

I swore to them that as far as I knew, Janice was alive and living in California and I didn't have no explanation for why she hadn't contacted her Mama and Daddy during all these years. I reckon most of my family thought that if I was honest enough to admit that I had killed Patricia Ann, I might be telling the truth about Janice, which of course I wasn't.

Like I already admitted, the body in the grave I took the law to, the body I said was Janice was really a girl I had picked up outside Columbia. She was from Minnesota. Her name was Freeman or something like that. I'll tell more about her later. As for Janice, she truly died the way I have just told it.

I know that admitting all this now, so many years later, is bound to upset my sister and her family and lots of others, but what gets written here is my last chance to say what really happened. It all has got to be told now with no more of my lies. This is the final truth that I promised everything in this book would be.

10

In December of 1970, the month after I killed Janice and Patricia Ann, the law's attention got pulled away from their case by the murder of a thirteen year old girl named Peggy Cuttino.

But lawmen couldn't treat her the same way they had Janice's and Patty's case, like just another fart that would soon blow away, because Peggy Cuttino's daddy was a prominent man, powerful in politics. Besides that, whoever killed Peggy had left her body where it was sure to be found so the law couldn't get away with saying she was probably just another runaway. In this case, law men had to do something fast or they would end up in deep political shit and they knew it.

So the law went to work to find a criminal mind to do the time. They had watched me ever since I got questioned in Sumter, still they hadn't ever got nothing on me because they didn't know shit about the tenant house and my car works or coastal killings or anything else.

But in the Cuttino case, they needed an ex-con with a record that included hard time and killing, a murder in CCI would do, so they decided Pee Wee Gaskins satisfied their needs nearabout perfectly. Howsomever, if they thought I'd lie down easy and spread my cheeks, they had another thing coming. My education come later in life than most, but my professors was the best.

They picked me up and I was questioned by all the law. The local police, county deputies, and the South Carolina State law Enforcement Division, SLED. I expected the fucking Marines to show up next. But I had an alibi they couldn't bust. I could prove I was in Charleston when Peggy Cuttino took missing and I could account for every hour of my time from then until they found her body.

One of the SLED Agents said he didn't believe me because such a tight alibi had to be rigged because nobody normal could account for every hour like I could. I acted real offended and said I wasn't just some normal prick and they damn well couldn't fuck me over just any old way they wanted. I demanded to take a polygraph lie detector test, which was give me in the public defender's office and which I passed, like I always do, and they turned me loose.

That was when one of the law men told some reporters we have questioned Pee Wee Gaskins and released him because his alibi checks out. Then an out of town news man asked who Pee Wee Gaskins was and the lawman said Pee Wee is a small time punk who talks and acts tough to get women to notice him but that's all he is, just talk. Later the same lawman said he had seriously underestimated Gaskins. I reckon that sure as shit stinks, he truly did.

It took a while longer before the law suddenly discovered that a man named William Junior Pierce was the criminal they had been looking for all the time. He had been in the Sumter area when Peggy took missing and had left there at about the time her body was found.

lawmen testified once they was reminded that they surely did remember seeing him in the county and town. Not long after Peggy's murder, Pierce had been arrested over in Georgia and convicted of what the law said was perpetration of a similar type crime. He was pulling life there when the South Carolina law decided he suited their purposes in the Cuttino case.

They brought him to trial to quieten down the public, and press, and politicians who was all raising hell because so much time was going by and nobody had been arrested and made to pay for Peggy's death. The judge sealed the autopsy evidence to spare the family the publicity of the torture done to her.

The rest of the evidence was circumstantial and there weren't much of that. But Junior never had no chance at all of getting any justice. The jury found him guilty and the judge tacked another life sentence onto the one Junior was serving. If he ever gets parole in Georgia they will bring him to South Carolina to start his sentence here.

final truth. Junior Pierce did not kill Peggy Cuttino. I did.

Seven years later, during my trial for murdering Barnwell Yates, I admitted I killed Peggy, but I was ignored by the court because they already had Pierce doing life for killing her. Then a year later, in '78, when I plea bargained myself eight life sentences in place of another sure ticket to the chair, I confessed again to killing Peggy.

The way that second confession come about was like this. judge David Harwell and prosecutor Kenneth Summerford, who I called Old Double Barrel, cause he always took aim at me with both bores loaded, asked me to go to McLeod Memorial Hospital and be questioned under sodium amytal in order to verify the crimes I had confessed to as part of the plea bargain deal.

As far as I was concerned, that truth serum was the same as another polygraph test, so I agreed to do it. I took the serum, and I shoveled the same shit at the hospital as I always shoveled for the law, which included my own lawyers. I never knew one who I could trust with the final truth, so I never gave it to any of them. I'll tell more about what I think of lawyers later.

The point here is that I put Peggy Cuttino on my list of murder victims and I verified her under the truth serum, but damned if the law enforcement officers didn't say that I had lied about killing Peggy and they took her off the list. When the law was asked about all this later, they told the press the Cuttino case is closed. Gaskins included her name in order to get publicity.

I said it then, and I still say it, bullshit! Think about it, it don't make no sense, why would I want more publicity? Admitting more murders sure wasn't going to help me none. I confessed because I knowed Junior Pierce weren't guilty and I didn't want him to end up in South Carolina's CCI for a crime he didn't commit.

As for the real reason why Old Double Barrel Summerford and Sumter solicitor Kenneth Young, who prosecuted Junior Pierce, didn't accept my confession, the onliest thing that I can say is that I truly didn't understand why. Maybe somebody ought to ask them. All I'm sure about is that even though Junior Pierce done other crimes, he weren't guilty of killing Peggy Cuttino, and the law knowed it.

Now that I've said all that, I want to tell what truly happened to Peggy Cuttino, which was this. In December of 1970 I was working for Fort Roofing & Sheet Metal Company, doing repairs at the school.

My bothersomeness had been coming on for a day or two and I needed to get to the coast as soon as I could. It was late, almost quitting time, and I was outside by the truck getting a few tools when I seen Peggy and a couple of her friends walking on the sidewalk toward me. I guess they must have come back for books or something, school was out by then.

I knowed Peggy, leastwise I surely knowed who she was, her Daddy was a real respected man, so when her and her friends walked by, not more than six foot away from where I was standing, I said, "hello, Peggy," and I smiled real polite, and she stuck her nose in the air like she smelled something, and turned on her heels, and didn't speak to me, and when they was walking away I heard one of her friends say, "who was that?" And Peggy said, "just white trash, can't you tell?"

Now there just weren't no call for that. But I knowed better than to say anything back to her, even though I was real pissed off. Howsomever, it surely stayed with me. After I got off work I stopped at a club and almost got into three fights in a half hour. I was hurting bad. I needed the coast. I started driving after dark and got to Charleston in the middle of the night and took a room at the tourist camp where I usually stayed, one of them where most customers rent by the hour.

Next day I went looking for hitch hikers and picked up one about noon. I didn't finish with her until almost sundown. I just kept wanting to do more and more, to make her hurt worser and worser. When she finally sank, the relief was good. I stayed the next night in Charleston and went to my favorite seafood restaurant, then to a club where I knew folks.

I was feeling lots better, though I still couldn't get that little miss Peggy bitch, and what she had said, out of my head. That's when I telephoned my foreman and told him I was in Charleston talking to somebody about going into business there, and I wouldn't be back for a few days, and he said he would cover for me, which was real good because I wanted everybody to know that I was in Charleston.

I paid for the tourist cabin in advance. I came and went a lot on purpose, then I drove back to Sumter and parked not too far from the Cuttino house and got out and hid and watched and waited and like some other times in my life my luck come with my patience. All of a sudden, there she was.

I grabbed her, clamped my hand over her mouth, and pressed the knife blade flat on her neck. She didn't scream, but she did piss her panties. I handcuffed her, and put ducting tape over her mouth, and put her in the trunk. I spent a long time with Miss Peggy in the barn where I did my car work. I spread her on a work table and raped her and burned her and did lots of other things before I killed her.

I had planned to take her body to the coast and bury her in the marshes with the others, and be seen in some more places around Charleston to air tighten my alibi, but it come to me that maybe Peggy was one body I shouldn't bury.

The papers was full of her disappearing, and I knew that the law wouldn't never quit looking for her. Her family was too important and well knowed. And while lawmen was searching, the dumb asses might accidentally stumble onto bodies or stole cars or something else connected to me that I would rather be left unfound. It would be better all around, I figured, if they stopped looking, so

I dumped her where she was sure to be found. Then I drove back to Charleston.

I got a special purpose in going on so much about all this. I want to prove to the judge and to Old Double Barrel and to anybody else stupid enough to believe that Junior Pierce is guilty and Pee Wee Gaskins needs publicity that I am the one that's telling everything straight this time around. My final truth is true. Theirs is the lie.

Proof that what I say here is true don't take but a few words. Reports before and during Junior Pierce's trial said that Peggy Cuttino's body was covered with cigarette torture burns, but no more details was ever made known because, like I already said, the official report weren't never released for the family's sake.

So it's logical to say that the onliest person outside of the coroner and court officials who knows the truth about them burns is the one who did the torture and the murder. And that weren't Junior Pierce. And them burns weren't made with no cigarettes. I poured acid on her, a trickle at a time.

11

By the time 1971 got here, the law was paying more attention to me than made me comfortable. Two years of my parole was finished so I could go into Florence County again, but that just meant two sheriffs and even more deputies was watching so I decided that because of the foregoings on in November and December, I ought to make some changes in my life, at least as far as what the law could see.

First thing I did, the first day of the new year, was get married. I knowed our marriage weren't legal cause I was still married to a few others, but she was pregnant and I wanted her to stay with me.

Second thing I did, in June, not long after our boy was born, was start working at Kolb's Used Cars, rebuilding clunkers. That way it looked normal when I carried around auto parts in my car. With my new work there and my new wife and baby, I didn't spend much time at the tenant house, usually only when a out of state car come in for me to strip and repaint. My deal with the two guys I had knowed in CCI kept going smooth. The law never got a hint of what we was doing because we hardly never met up so we weren't seen together. They brought the cars from Georgia on backroads and left them hid in some pine woods near Roper's Crossroads, which is a place just like its name says, where two roads cross and there is a country store. My daughter, and her husband, and kids lived near there, and they never knew that my visits with them was also to pick up cars left close by. The keys was in the car ashtray and any cash due me was in a paper sack under the back seat and I brought back the redid cars with parts in the trunk the same way. In three years nobody ever messed with them cars or stole any parts or money.

Even before I quit construction to work at Kolb's Used Cars, I had gave up dealing stole property with them reefer dopehead boys. Doing business with them was too risky. If the law ever popped them I knew they'd roll over on me fast as a pig squirts shit. I was making good money reworking cars at the tenant barn so I didn't need to take no more chances than I already took.

I still got my regular painful needs and went to the coast for a day or two. I told my wife I just had to get away from everybody every once in a while, the same as I needed to go out and hang around honkytonks on occasion, or needed a strange piece now and again. I made that understood with all the women I ever lived with. Like I said, they all put up with me in spite of whatever I done. I never could figure out whether it was because they truly loved me that much or because they was all that afraid of me.

I have a notion that most women who were ever around me for very long got a sixth sense about the violence inside me. Fact is, there was one woman who said she got real scared whenever I come because my come smelled and tasted of death. But I'll tell more about Suzanne later.

In those days I never give no thought to stopping doing coastal kills. They was a clock kind of thing. When it was time, I went and killed. I had it all worked out, real efficient, pick up to burial. I kept on thinking up new things to do. My best ideas still usually come when I was in hardware stores or working on a car and holding one tool or another in my hand. And during all of 1971 nothing much changed as far as coastal kills was concerned except for one time that summer when I picked up two girls together, which I hadn't never done before. And I weren't at all sure it was a good idea when I did it, considering the problems I had trying to handle Janice and Patricia Ann both at the same time.

But I usually learn from problems so when I picked up these two, I didn't waste no time. Soon as I surprised them with the pistol, I put the cuffs and duct tape on them without giving them no chance to try to get away, or attack me, or anything like that. It worked real good. Afterwards I was happy I had gone ahead and done it. There was something special about having one girl watch what I did to the other one, knowing her turn was coming. Then the other one, already hurting, watching and knowing I was coming back to her. And the most surprising thing to me was that after they sank I felt a kind of double peacefulness, better than any ever before.

Counting them two, I did eleven coastal kills in '71, which, of course, don't include that year's serious murders.

Martha Ann Clyde Dicks use to come around the car lot and talk to anybody who would listen. She was a loud bitch who thought she was something special because she had done two years in reform school, smoked reefer, got high on pills, and ate pussy. She was tall, and strong, and tough, and called herself Clyde to let folks know she was lesbianese. But in my opinion, she had already been give the right name, Dicks, cause if ever there was a bitch who thought she had a dick, it was Clyde.

Now don't get me wrong, I surely understand what the sight and smell and taste of pussy can do to a person so I don't blame Clyde and her kind for liking to lick and suck each other and all that. But for women to do it to women just don't seem right. The way it's intended, women is supposed to get fucked and eat out by men. Of course playing the dyke game in prison where there ain't always a dick handy is understandable. That's the same as a man in prison having to settle for a mustached mouth and muscle ass.

I am explaining all this because I don't want anybody to get the idea it was any kind of prejudice that led me to murder Clyde. I didn't kill her cause she was black. Of course, it's a straight fact that she was black, a purple tongue we used to call them. But I never killed nobody because of their race. I admit I growed up in a part of the state notable through the years for the activities of the Ku Klux Klan, and in my life I have been to some Klan rallies and meetings and I have favored some positions took by the Klan on some issues, but I have never beat up or flogged or killed anybody just because they was black.

I killed Clyde because she was a God damned loud mouthed liar who made the mistake of telling her lies about me and thinking they was funny. She showed up at Kolb's Used Cars two or three times a week in the late afternoon. She didn't live far away, some place off of Manning Street. There was usually a bunch of men and boys hanging around the garage and Clyde didn't make no bones about the fact that when she and her girlfriend was in need of bread for shit and droppers she was willing to suck or fuck for five dollars.

Sometimes she opened her shirt and showed her tits to tease the guys hanging around or pulled down her jeans and showed her shaved pussy and laughed and said, "where there ain't no bushes, no crabs can hide." And she bragged she could suck a two inch ball bearing through a half inch pipe and them that had gone with her said she did give one mean heavy sucking blowjob.

Actually, I didn't mind Clyde hanging around. The fact was I liked listening to her. She was funny, real entertaining. But all of a sudden, for some reason I never did understand, she started in messing with me. At first it was all kindly kidding, saying things like she wanted Pee Wee and Dicks to get together. Everybody laughed at remarks like that including me.

But then she started saying things like she sure enjoyed last night with Pee Wee, and that Pee Wee really fills me up and I thought my girlfriend knew how to eat pussy until I let Pee Wee suck me. Even them remarks might have been okay if she had let off after awhile, but the more the fellows around the garage laughed, the more worser things she thought up to say the next time she was there.

finally, I had enough. I asked her to stay around one evening and when we was alone I told her that I didn't want no problems with her, but I thought she had made me the ass end of her jokes too often and I wanted her to stop or pick somebody else. She said, "I would tell you to suck my ass, Pee Wee, but you'd probably like the taste of my shit so much I couldn't get rid of you." Then she shot me a bird and walked out.

Clyde didn't come around for a couple of weeks after that, and I thought maybe she had decided to stay away for good, but I was wrong. She had gone to Atlanta with her girlfriend and when she come back she weren't funny at all anymore. She started off by saying, in front of everybody, that she was pregnant with a little Pee Wee and that whether I married her or not she was going to name the baby after me, Pee Wee Dicks.

That was more than I could tolerate. I got a feeling some of the men was thinking there truly was something between me and Clyde and I couldn't allow that. I laughed and kidded the best I could for the rest of that afternoon then I told Clyde I needed to talk to her again and she stayed around after closing time like she wasn't scared of me one damn little bit.

I acted real nice and told her I had some yellow jackets and red devils I would give her in exchange for one of her famous blowjobs and an assfuck. I said that since she was telling everybody I had done it with her, I might as well find out if she was good as she said she was, but I didn't want to do it in the garage, I wanted to go to my place. The stupid bitch said okay and we drove to the Tenant house.

I wasn't about to take no chances with her. I knew she was strong and quick so I stayed calm and handed her a plastic bottle full of all different kinds of pills I had got out of the purses of some of my coastal kills. I didn't know what they was but Clyde did and right off she swallowed a handful with a beer. Soon she was high, drunk, buck naked, singing and dancing around the room and finally falling across the bed. I didn't specially like the idea of that even though I knew I could take the covers off later and get them washed.

When she laughed and told me to get naked I took off my shirt, and rolled her on her stomach, and snapped on the handcuffs before she even knew I had them. She jumped up and commenced to cussing. I punched her jaw and knocked her to the floor. When she started to get up, I kicked her in the face with my boot. Then I held the bottle of pills to her mouth and made her swallow every last one of them with swigs of beer.

When she looked at me, I didn't have to tell her she was going to die, she knew it but I told her anyhow. She layed there real quiet, her eyes wide, while I pinched her tits and poked and examined her privates and sniffed but didn't taste.

I didn't have to wait long until she was unconscious. I tried to pick her up, but she was too much for me to lift and carry so I dragged her outside and shoved her into the back seat of the car. It was dark by the time l headed out highway fifteen toward five-twenty-one.

I was almost to the intersection when I met a highway patrol car and recollected how them smoky hats always pleasured they selfs in stopping me for no reason but to harass me so I turned onto the back roads and headed to a farm where I knew there was plenty of deep drainage ditches. Before we got there, Clyde had messed herself and stank real bad and I knew she were dead.

I weighted her and dumped her in a ditch then wrapped her clothes around rocks and threw them in beside her. I drove back to the tenant house and cleaned the stink of her out of my car. It was so bad it took me near about two hours to do it.

What I'm hoping is that this final truth about Clyde Dicks makes it real clear that I didn't kill her for no reason besides her lying mouth. Not because she was black or because she were lesbianese and damn sure not because she was pregnant by me.

Two things is sworn facts. I'm not prejudiced against no particular race, creed, or color, and I never in my whole life put my dick in no black pussy.

When I picked her up, the girl told me her name were Anne Colberson. At least that's the way it sounded, I'm not too good at spelling. She was a pretty thing, kind of skinny, with the biggest blackest eyes I ever seen on any girl in my life, excepting maybe that one on television. In most ways this was like a simple coastal kill except that when I picked her up hitching outside Myrtle Beach I weren't feeling bothersome and I weren't driving coast roads looking for hitch hikers. I was just driving back to Sumter after leaving my wife and son at the beach to spend two weeks with some friends.

She said she was from Georgia and had been to Myrtle Beach on a house party, which is what kids call getting together all in one house at the beach and drinking beer and the girls prick teasing the boys who ain't got nothing but one thing on they minds. She said she had rid the bus to the beach the week before and she had bus fare home, but she was saving up to buy something so decided to hitchhike to Atlanta where her boyfriend was to meet her at the bus station downtown.

I remembered the bus station because that was where the guards had took me to the bus when I got released from federal. I told her I knew where the bus station was and that by a strange coincidence I was driving to Atlanta to start work on a new job there and I would be happy to give her a ride all the way. She smiled real big and said this sure was her lucky day and I knowed it was mine.

She talked to me real nice. Her friends were all at the beach for the whole month, but she had to go back because she had a summer job and only got one week off. She was sixteen and her boyfriend was seventeen and played football. In fact, he had been at football camp the week she had been to the beach. I don't remember the town she said she was from but I do remember that as we was riding up the highway she said something about having lots of relatives in Atlanta.

The longer we rode and talked, and the more I got a chance to look her over, the more I knew I had made a good decision. It was special nice to be with a pretty girl without feeling painful and bothersome inside, without feeling any need, just anticipating.

When we turned off the highway onto country back roads leading to the tenant house and barn, she asked where we was going and I told her I knowed this area real good and we was taking a short cut to go around Columbia. I said that if she liked, in a little while we could stop at a place I knew that served the best barbecue anywhere.

When we stopped at the tenant house it was too late for her. She started to say something, but I drew out my Beretta and pointed it at her. That always scares them into being real quiet, like their first look of the toothpick always makes them piss.

I kept Anne Colberson with me four days and nights. That's the longest I recollect ever keeping any of them. She were a sweet girl. She did everything I asked her to and never fought me or cussed me or called me names and the onliest times she yelled and cried was when I cut her and pushed things deep in her.

In a way, I begun to feel real fond of her. I never got agitated or bothersome or angered at her. I just felt calm and peaceful and joyed. I never meant to be mean to her. I was just pleasuring myself. Though I could tell from her screaming that the things I done must've hurt a powerful lot, specially when I plugged her pee hole with plumbum and things like that.

When she had screamed long as I cared to hear, I hit her with the peen just hard enough to knock her out and end her pain because she had been so nice to me. Then I went to dig, and when I come back, I took off the handcuffs and dressed her, then I carried her out, and laid her in her grave, and cut her throat, and listened to the red gurgling, and I hoped she wouldn't wake up and suffer. And she didn't.

I buried her near where I buried Janice. I sank her clothes and suitcase in the same swamp spot near the neck where I had sank Janice's and Patricia Ann's purses.

When '71 was close to ending, I got the feeling that if I stayed around Sumter much longer even its dick brained lawmen was likely to stumble onto something I was doing. They might follow me and find out about the tenant house and barn and come back with a search warrant. And though I weren't real fearful they would find the bodies buried there because they didn't have no reason to look for no bodies, it came down to more than just a matter of me not wanting to get caught for murder.

I didn't want to get caught and go back to prison for car stripping, stole property, or nothing else, not ever.

And, like I said, I was getting this feeling every time I took a car to the barn or delivered a repainted one with its trunk full of parts, that the law was sniffing a mite closer. So I decided to move away from Sumter. wwwCharleston was my choice. I had got to know some people and places there and I liked it. It was a big city, the biggest in South Carolina. It was different from the little towns where I was used to living, but the people were my kind, low country folks who are the best there is. I checked out possible jobs and even found an old garage that was near about perfect for stripping and rebuilding cars.

We moved to North Charleston in '72. Right off I got a job with Picquet Construction and I did part time work at a couple of auto garages and averaged one car stripping a week. It was good money though there was more things to spend money on in Charleston than in Sumter and most things there cost a lot more.

Of course, the real reason I picked Charleston was so I could be close to the coast roads I needed to ride when the bothersomeness come. Living there, I could travel them even when the pain weren't around, when I just wanted to go out and pleasure myself. Because coastal killing had got easier, I did more that year.

And I did two serious murders in 1972.

Soon after I moved to Charleston, one of the men who brought me stole cars from out of state come to see me where I worked, which was a surprise cause we had agreed we wouldn't never be seen together, that's why we still had a system of him dropping off cars and me picking them up, like we done in Sumter, except instead of parking them in the woods, now we used a shopping center.

Anyhow, as I was saying, he come to see me and said he wanted me to meet a young guy he had cell mated with for a few months in the Richmond

County Jail, which is Augusta, Georgia. He said the guy was black and was heavy into stole property and, since we both lived in Charleston, he thought maybe we could do some good business with each other.

That's how I met Eddie Brown who was one huge man, or a real big motherfucker as he called hisself. He was also one hell of a good man. Him and me hit it off from the start. I never did have much luck with blacks in CCI and most of the ones I worked with in construction in Sumter stayed shy of me, though I never give'em any real reason to. What Eddie was heavy into weren't just any old stole property, Eddie was into stole guns. He bought and sold. Who he sold to, he never said and I never asked. Weren't none of my business. All I know is he done real well at it. He drove a Lincoln which, though it weren't brand new, weren't but two years old and still had the new smell inside.

Eddie had just turned twenty-four the year I knew him and he was married to the longest legged, best looking black girl I ever saw. If I ever got a hardon over a black woman, it was for Bertie Brown. To tell it straight, no lie, she could have been in the movies. I liked them both so much that one time I actually invited them to my house for dinner when my wife wasn't there. She weren't too I fond of being around blacks so I kept her separated from Eddie and Bertie much as I could. I enjoyed having them to my house. I brought in barbeque ribs and beer and we had a nice evening. By then we had been doing deals for a few months.

I had put the word out where I worked that I bought guns no questions asked, if they was the right price. I got quite a few that way and I noticed that Eddie was always quick to pay me more for semi-rifles and automatic handguns. That was when I hit on a better idea. I started hanging around beer joints near the Navy base and some weekends, when I took my wife to visit her folks near Sumter, I drove to Columbia and hung around joints near Fort Jackson and did the same around Shaw Air Force Base right there at Sumter. In all them places I let it be knowed that I was looking for military weapons for collectors. The results was amazing. Most times I ended up buying six or eight military weapons. And whatever I paid apiece for them, I sold them to Eddie for double and God knows what he got for them.

That' s when I found out that fully automatics was worth more than semis so I set up a work bench in my house and learned to convert them. It's damned simple. There's five parts of the firing mechanism that needs changing and the parts comes in repair kits. A little time and know how and I could get four times what I had paid for the weapon. It was even better than the car business. Until Eddie got picked up for questioning by the ATF Feds who had seized a hundred rifles being loaded from a truck onto a boat at Sullivan's Island Marina. Most of the guns had been stole from the military. And somehow the feds connected them to Eddie. He said later that he figured the truck driver rolled on him. Soon as the feds let him loose, Eddie called me from a pay phone near his house and said he needed to buy more guns real quick to sell to raise cash so he could afford to hire the onliest lawyer who could guarantee to get him out of the truly deep shit he knowed he was in.

It was just a matter of time, he said, before the feds showed up with a warrant to arrest him. He knew that from the way they had questioned him. He said he could advance me three thousand dollars to do my buying if I would help him. I thought fast and said I would be happy to help him out and that I didn't need any front money. I had some cash, I said and I would buy as many weapons for him as I could. But I told him I didn't want to deliver them in Charleston. It was too easy for the feds to follow him in the city. We should meet out in the country where he could shake loose any tails that the feds might decide to put on him.

Eddie agreed and asked where and when we could meet. I told him I could have the guns in two days and I gave him the directions to Sumter and told him where to turn off of the main road to get to the tenant house. Soon as I was off the phone, I went into my work room and got all my tools plus the three rifles I had just converted and put them in my car trunk. Then I got my wife and boy and we headed for Sumter.

I left them with her folks and I stayed at my daughter's mobile home that night. Next day I went to the tenant house. I had took everything out before I moved to Charleston. I had not left even the leastest bit of evidence there. I had even took all the locks off the doors and tore out the plumbing so it would be too ramshackle for anybody to ever want to live in. In spite of all that, I still checked and made sure nobody was around. Then I spent a couple of hours getting things ready, after which I went back to my daughter's and played with my grand kids the rest of the day. That evening I went honkytonking.

Next afternoon late I was back at the tenant house when Eddie and Bertie got there. He was smart. Instead of driving that big new Lincoln, he was driving a plain '61 brown Ford that sounded like it run good but looked like a rusted turd. They was both nervous. He said they had left Charleston after breakfast, drove all the way to Savannah, then up to Columbia and down to Sumter to make sure nobody followed them. The way Eddie talked it were purely plain to me that he weren't near as tough as he made out to be and I knew that my decision, made spur on the moment when he first called and told me about the feds, was the right decision.

I told him and Bertie that the guns was in the barn and I led the way. I had stashed one automatic rifle with a thirty clip on a shelf just inside the door, another clip was tucked in my belt. Soon as I got in the barn I picked up the rifle, chambered a round, turned, and before they could say or do shit, I opened fire.

Because he was the bigger danger, I emptied almost the full clip into him. The stream of fire damn near cut him in half. Only a few hit Bertie, but they was enough to tear open her crotch. She fell to the ground and tried to crawl away but was too hurt to go far. I changed clips, then decided not to shoot no more.

Instead, I went to my car and got the toothpick and walked back to her. She was staring at Eddie who was lying real still, tore open from neck to dick, guts spilling out. Then she looked up at me and started soft crying but didn't say nothing. I grabbed her ankles and dragged her to the edge of the hole I had dug on yesterday. Then I turned loose her legs, and grabbed her hair, and cut her throat, and rolled her into the grave.

Getting him there weren't that easy. It was hard even to drag him because he was so big and messy and slimy. His intestines trailed behind us all the way from the barn. finally, I got him to the grave and pushed him in on top of her. Then I had to spend more than an hour shoveling spadefuls of dirt, and guts, and blood, and putting them in the hole until at last everything was cleaned up and I had them buried deep and proper like I wanted.

Killing them were a matter of it being necessary. He was a good man and she hadn't never been anything but nice and friendly to me, but I knowed that once the feds charged him and leaned on him heavy about where he got them automatic weapons and then started talking a deal with him, he would rollover on me without giving it no second thoughts.

I knowed from experience that that was just the way things was. But if I could help it, I wasn't going back to prison, even to federal, just because some real big mother fucker turned out to be a really big piece of chicken shit. I reckon killing them two qualified as a serious murder because I did know them and I did bury them both back of the barn not far from Janice and pretty little Anne, but they didn't really mean shit to me. They could've just as easy been coastal kills.

12

I never got any visits from the ATF feds asking about weapons. A Charleston deputy did come by one evening asking if I knew Eddie and Bertie Brown. I said I barely knowed them, didn't even know where they lived, and for sure didn't have no idea where they could be found. The deputy seemed satisfied with my answers. Leastwise he never come back.

And good as the gun business had been, I figured it wasn't worth shit without Eddie so I had best just leave it alone. I took my last three rifles and my conversion kits, along with the three guns I found in Eddie's car, and his wallet and Bertie's purse, and sank them all in my favoritest swamp spot near The Neck. I kept Eddie's car just long enough to change its color from turd brown to dark blue then I sent it out of state to sell.

By Spring '73 I had got to know lots of people in Charleston, most of them connected through somebody they knowed in CCI. I also knew plenty of women I'd met at clubs and tonks and folks from Sumter and Florence always looked me up whenever they was in Charleston. So most evenings our house was full of folks visiting.

When we first moved to North Charleston I had noticed that my bothersomeness was coming as regular monthly as a woman's rag time and it always let me know a few days ahead when to expect it. I got nervous by the tenth, edgy and mean by the twelfth, and the pains commenced on the fourteenth or fifteenth. Years later I read about that women's PMS-thing and I reckoned that what I had was pre murdering signals. My relief still come only with coastal kills

In winter time, searching and finding weren't all that easy. More than a few times I had to drive south clear past Jacksonville to find a hitcher who looked right. And because I didn't know north Florida real good, I couldn't take chances so soon as I picked one up, I pulled off the Highway, and drew my pistol, and cuffed and taped her, and put her in the trunk and drove straight back to South Carolina. I felt safer doing my killing and burying in my home state. I guess I'm just a Carolina southern boy at heart.

In June of '73, on my little boy's second birthday. we went to the Isle of Palms beach and I remember laying on the sand and thinking that all in all my life was pretty damn good. Then in July, wham, a lightning bolt shot straight up my ass. Some son of a bitch, or maybe it were just some bitch, burned down my house. Plain to see and smell, the fire weren't no accident. We were in Sumter for the weekend when it broke out and we lost everything we owned except the clothes we had with us. And I didn't carry insurance because that was something I never believed in.

There was a number of people on my suspect list, male and female, who was royal pissed off at me about something I had done or not done to them or for them. For example, I had had arguments, time to time, with some guys about money from stole property and cars. I thought I was always fair when it come to dividing the cash, allowing as I did for my expenses and risk taking, but not everybody always agreed with my figures and several times I had to draw my Beretta to get my point took. And if money and deals weren't enough trouble, there was always some bitch or other who didn't like the way I treated her after we fucked. Some even got mad enough to tell their husbands or boyfriends.

For whatever the reason, there was damn sure somebody red ass mad enough at me right then to burn down my house. That was why I decided that we ought to move away from Charleston for a while. My wife liked the idea, so we moved back to the Florence. Sumter area. Fact is, we moved to the community of Prospect which is spitting distance from where I growed up at Leo. We lived in a little apartment in back of Todd's Grocery Store which was the center of Prospect in that there was three buildings in prospect and it was the one in the middle.

Alongside the store was a fishing pond, not real big, maybe an acre or two, covered with green slime. Years later, when lawmen asked me if anybody I knowed was at the bottom of that pond, I said no, the only scum I knowed in Prospect weren't on, or in, no pond, and that was the truth. Why would I bury anybody right outside my door when there was hundreds and hundreds of acres of swamp bogs all around that area?

Living in Prospect didn't mean I moved everything there. I did some work in Florence County, but I still kept my contacts and deals and stripping going in Charleston and went back and forth regular, which fitted in real well with coastal kills. We lived in Prospect six months, until the end of '73 and I did three serious murders during that time there.

Jackie Freeman was the runaway I told a little about earlier on. It was her grave I took lawmen to and said that that was where I had buried my niece, Janice Kirby. I picked up Jackie in October of '73, just another one of my good fortune things. I had gone to Columbia to sell some stole items I got the week before from two boys in Lake City who wasn't dopeheads and I was on my way home when I seen her.

She was small, mainly because she was real young. Fourteen, she said, and that was what she looked. She was from some place way the hell up north in Minnesota. She said it snowed there a lot. I asked her if she came to Carolina to get warm and she said she had run away from home because her hateful stepdaddy was always doing things to her, which I took to mean he raped her, and I said I sure understood all about hating stepdaddies. But when I looked at her, I knew how her stepdaddy must've felt living in the house with such tender stuff. I offered to take her lo Myrtle Beach and she seemed real grateful of course. I didn't have no intention of doing what I offered.

When I first moved back to Prospect, I had checked out the tenant house and found out that a black family had rented the place or was buying it. I never asked no details because if anything was ever found there I didn't want it connected to me. All that meant to me right then was that I had to find a different place real quick to take this Jackie girl so I drove to an abandoned house near Prospect not too far from our old Hideout. It didn't have no electricity or water, but I didn't need them, I had a lantern and flashlights plus my rope and chains and duct tape and a little plumbum stove and all.

I held the toothpick on Jackie and she stripped. Then I cuffed her and tied her up real tight and gagged her and put her in the trunk, and drove to a grocery store and bought enough food and soft drinks for the two of us. Then we went back to the vacant house. Because there weren't no agitating in me, I could go real slow and enjoy just pure pleasuring with this girl. I liked that. Not even the fact she was minnie-strating bothered me. I just pulled the string and unplugged her, which gave her more to lick clean after I corned, which I enjoyed up front because of that.

It was while I was heating the plumbum that I got my different idea. I used the toothpick to slice and the plumber's fire to cook, and I didn't share like I did with that first girl. It was strange flavored cooked real good, though I think maybe it was more the idea than the taste. Whichever, it were enough to make me decide to try other parts of her.

I kept her there a couple of days. It would've been longer if she hadn't cried and whimpered all the time. That got on my nerves so right after dark the second night I duct taped her and took her to the car and drove to a swamp trail I knew off highway three-four-one and cut her throat and buried her.

I did such a good job of hiding her that when I led lawmen to her, to show them what I said was Janice's grave, I had a hard time finding it myself. Because

I brought her to Prospect, and knew and remembered her name, and I guess you could say because she had became part of me, I always thought of Jackie as special, not really a serious murder, but likewise not just another coastal kill.

The weekend after I buried Jackie, I drove more trails around Prospect and the Neck, which is a special place near there where some truly fine folks live, and where even lawmen is generally scared shitless to go after dark. The people there don't take kindly to anybody but their own. I've got good friends and kin there and I was getting to know more folks and finding new places I might need sooner or later. That same weekend, something real strange happened.

I was doing shade tree work for a fellow who wanted to be a stock car driver and needed help pulling an engine, when another fellow we knew come by driving a Cadillac hearse. He had bought it cheap, he said, and figured to sell it for a pretty good profit, but nobody wanted the damned thing. It was like people was afraid to drive a hearse because dead bodies had been in it. Well, let me tell you, I bought that hearse on the spot right then and there for next to nothing, less than what he had paid for it.

I never could get my wife to ride in it with me, but I drove that sucker everywhere.

I had a sign made that said, "we haul anything, living or dead," and I put it in the back window. The first time I drove it to Charleston, everybody kidded me about it, and it soon become a running kind of joke. Everybody said, "hey, Pee Wee, why you driving a hearse?" And I said, "because I kill so many people, I need a hearse to haul them to my private cemetery." Then we would all laugh. But I knew them guys who knew my reputation from CCI was whispering to the others that I really was a killer. It's funny, but when an ex-con knows you've murdered, he tells his friends like some of your made bones reputation might rub off on him. I got the same reactions at clubs and tonks in Sumter and Florence and Lake City and Johnsonville. Anyplace I went.

Even lawmen kidded me about that hearse. Every time deputies saw me somewhere they started with that same hearse, cemetery joking around. Then word got back to me that all them lawmen thought I was funny and was calling me crazy little Pee Wee Gaskins, which suited the shit out of me. As long as they was laughing at me, I knew they weren't likely suspecting me of being involved in nothing serious.

Apart from all that, I have to say that I got more ass in the back of that hearse than in any vehicle I ever owned. Fucking a stone killer in the back of a hearse truly turned on them women who liked the smell of violence and death. Of course, I didn't push my luck too far. I never took the hearse on my coastal drives. I didn't figure the kind of girls I was looking for would like the idea too much. Besides, a hearse was too easy to remember. I didn't want its description to be a part of anybody's evidence. I always drove regular American cars on coastal kills. Fact is, I never did use the hearse to haul any corpses.

Until I did them two serious murders early in December of '73.

For reasons that gets apparent real soon, this here is the hardest murder for me to tell about. If the facts had got knowed too soon my life would have been a pure living hell. But in the end, because the end is coming real soon for me, all my final truth gets told here no matter what. So here goes.

I had knowed Doreen Dempsey a long time. Her stepdaddy and all his family worked with the carnival and lived in Sumter, that's how I got to know them. Doreen was adopted and give her folks an awful lot of grief. My wife had knowed her a long time before I ever did and once, when Doreen was on the outs with her folks about something, she come and stayed with us. That was when we lived in Sumter before we moved to Charleston, at about the time our son was born, and so Doreen helped take care of him them first few months.

Later, when Doreen got pregnant and went to that home of unwedded mothers in 1971, we went to see her. I guess you could say we was more than friends, in a way she was like part of our family. Her and her little girl, Robin Michelle, use to come to see us pretty often in Charleston where they also lived, but we hadn't heard nothing from her since we moved to Prospect.

Then one evening in December, Doreen, pregnant again, showed up in Prospect with two year old Robin and a son of a bitch named Johnny Sellars who I had done some previous deals with. It was a cold night, real windy. Doreen and Johnny drunk a couple of beers and stayed to supper and I remember little Robin Michelle climbing on Pee Wee's lap after we ate. She felt special good. I took a lap blanket from the couch and put it around her and she snuggled against me to keep warm.

Doreen said her and Robin needed a place to live until her next baby come, which looked like it could be any time. She said she was seven months but she looked more to me. I told her we just didn't have enough room in our little place for her and Robin, and me and my wife, and our son to all live. I suggested she ought to go on back to Charleston or to her stepmama's house in Sumter. Johnny Sellars said he had to go to Columbia later that night so he couldn't take her nowhere. A few minutes later he finished another beer and left. Doreen was real upset. I layed Robin Michelle on the sofa real gentle and tucked the blanket around her. Then I asked Doreen to take a walk with me.

Once we was outside, I told her that I didn't want my wife to hear, but I had a trailer near Roper's Crossroads where she and Robin could live rent free and I would give her some money to live on, but I expected regular servicing in return. She hugged me and said she didn't know what I wanted from a big fat pregnant girl like her, but whatever it was, I could have it.

Then we went back inside and, like we had arranged, she said she had decided to go back to Charleston on the bus and have her baby at Roper Hospital there. I told my wife I had give Doreen twenty dollars and was going to drive her to the bus station.

Doreen and Robin and me left in the hearse. After a few miles I drove off the main road, closer to Johnsonville than Prospect, and I told Doreen I wanted her to get naked and give me a blow job. She hesitated because Robin was watching, but finally she said okay and crawled in the back of the hearse and took off her clothes, which was a real job for a girl that pregnant.

Then I told her to hold her hands out in front of her and I put the handcuffs on her and she acted scared until I laughed and told her it was just a part of my sexy ways. She relaxed, and I told Robin to get in the back with her mama and I got naked and Doreen kneeled as best she could and commenced sucking.

Then I reached over and picked up Robin and started taking off her clothes. Doreen stopped what she was doing and asked me what the hell I was up to. I didn't reply nothing. I just picked up the ball peen hammer and popped her aside the head. She fell over sideways and lay still.

Robin started sobbing. I held her and said for her not to worry and not to cry because her mama was just sleeping. She got quiet and I finished undressing her and smelled and tasted of her. Then I made her take up where her mama had left off which took a lot of forcing, but finally she did what I said. Then I lifted her up and slid her down onto me, which made her scream real loud so I gagged her with her panties and duct tape.

It was like something over powerful was pushing me into that little thing. I couldn't stop. I needed real bad to feel my dick inside her, front and back. I choked her to death when I comed in her ass. It was the best and most over poweringest come I ever felt.

Doreen was still breathing. She was too fat for me to pick up and carry so I tied a rope around one of her legs and dragged her out of the hearse to a spot that looked soft and I dug a grave for her and her unborn baby and put them in it. Then I cut her throat and I covered the hole. I found a spot just big enough for Robin under a tree stump and buried her there. I told my wife and Doreen's friends and family that I had took her to the bus station in Florence and, far as I knew, Doreen and Robin was in Charleston. I never heard much else about them, least wise, the law never asked me nothing about them.

I know this here is not the way I told the story to Old Double Barrel Summerford, and my lawyers, and the judge, and everybody else when I plea bargained Doreen's and Robin's murders as a part of my deal five years later in 1978. But at that time, I was dealing for my life instead of the chair and I knew that beating execution again meant pulling even more life sentences so it was real important for me to tell a story that would convince the law that I was telling the truth, but at the same time wouldn't fuck up my reputation amongst the inmates at CCI.

I started out saying that I killed Doreen and Robin because I didn't have enough room for them to stay at my house, but it didn't appear that Prosecutor Summerford, and the judge, and lawyers was going to buy that so I told them that I drowned little Robin Michelle because she was half nigger and that I drowned Doreen for having one baby by a nigger and then getting pregnant by another nigger.

I knowed that since them men I was confessing to was all fine white southern gentlemen, they would surely believe I was telling the truth and understand my reasons when I said I killed Doreen and Robin because I was against any such mixing of the white and nigger races. And sure enough they accepted my story. And what was more important to me, I knew that the inmates at CCI would believe that story, at least the white inmates would, and they were the only ones who counted. Blacks has never been a part of my power inside, they just knowed better than to fuck with me.`

But like I keep saying, this here is my final truth, so let me make it clear. Killing Doreen and Robin didn't have nothing to do with her fucking niggers or her baby being half nigger. I told that story and made everybody believe it because I was going back to CCI and there weren't no way I could tell the truth and let it be knowed that I had killed Doreen and Robin to cover up what I had done to Robin.

If it had ever come out that I fucked that two year old girl front and back the inmates at CCI would have turned on me and refused me all respect. And no matter what bones I had made my reputation and power on the tiers and in the yard would have disappeared. And for me, surviving in CCI without respect and power would have been a whole lot worse than dying. I had to protect my reputation because reputation is all that men in prison, or outside for that matter, ever know about other men.

I don't expect many who read my words in this book to understand what I am saying. The plain and simple fact is that nobody can understand a man like me from reading and hearing. It takes experiencing it to understand it. And because most men won't never even allow their selves to find out what it's like even to just simple kill, much less to random torture and rape and murder, they can't never know what I know, that getting the guts and balls to do the first one just to pleasure yourself is the onliest difficult part. Once you've done the first, and come to know that real special feeling, you can't hardly wait until another better idea comes and leads and pulls and pushes you into what takes you up to another place even higher than you ever been before.

13

Those were my best years, years of freedom that never would have ever ended if I hadn't fucked up by trusting the wrong man. But I'll get to all that in proper order and time. We moved back to North Charleston the first week of January in '74. I left the hearse with friends in Sumter or Florence. I decided it was getting too identified with me. There were places I went where I didn't specially want people remembering seeing me. I still used the hearse time to time, long as I owned it, but not a whole lot.

In '74, I had so many things going on with so many different people I sometimes forgot who I was doing what with. First of all, there was my family and my wives's families and all their kin, plus the women and men in Sumter and Florence who come to visit and them that did the same in Charleston. And there was them that I did deals with, and boys that sold me stole property, and men who come recommended by nicknames from CCI.

I make a point of this because so many people are needed to tell *Final Truth* that it takes some doing to try to sort them out, and put names to faces, and make everything and everybody clear. I can remember the names of all my serious murder victims even the ones the law didn't know about, until now, but I'm not much help when it comes identifying coastal kills. To me they was victims without names buried in graves without markers. And even though I don't think I need to say this, I will. After I murdered Doreen and Robin Michelle, killing got even easier for me. So easy it was hard to tell when I done it to ease the bothersomeness and when I done it just to pleasure myself and when I killed somebody just because I decided they needed killing.

I still had the pains, Lord God knows I suffered mightily and needed relief, but I finally reached the point where I wanted the bothersomeness to start. I looked forward to it every month because it felt so good relieving myself of it. My coastal kills had all been girls up until 1974 when boys got included by a pure and simple accident.

It was March and cold as the balls on that brass monkey, or the tits on that witch, and there weren't hardly nobody out hitching. I figured I was in for a drive to Florida, then I saw the two of them, north of Savannah, hitching south. They was the kind that had packs on their backs and walked along the highway and half assed thumbed without turning round, like they didn't expect anybody would stop and didn't really much give a shit whether anybody did or not. They both had long straight hair and I would've swore they was girls. Course I couldn't see their asses because of their packs.

It weren't until I stopped and got out to open the Mustang's trunk that I seen they was boys. They was lean, skinny in fact, and was trying to sprout flimsy blond beards. They was fourteen they said when they was in the car and we headed south. They had met on the road, both runaways, so they had something in common right off, and they was going to Florida cause it was warm there. Neither one had any idea how they was going to live when they got there, they was just damned determined they wasn't ever going back home.

I said I sure understood what they was saying, I had done my share of running away when I was their age. But I warned them that they needed to be careful because Florida law was real tough on runaways. Besides, I added, they shouldn't never trust cops. That was how I had got sent to reformatory, trusting cops.

We talked along for a while until I saw a side road and turned down it. I had to stop, I said, because I had been having the trots and I needed to take a quick shit that couldn't wait. And soon as I stopped, I pulled the pistol and ordered them out. Just like girls, they got scared and quiet and done what I said. I cuffed them and taped their mouths, and moved their packs and my duffel from the trunk to the back seat, and put them both in the trunk, which was a tight fit, two teenage boys in a Mustang trunk.

I headed back north. It was late afternoon when we stopped on a trail I knew not far from Charleston. It was getting late and I knew I needed to work fast, but once I had them stripped and got a good look at them naked, I truly wanted to take my time. Not even in reform school did I remember seeing anything that tender looking. I had to have a smell and taste of them, and the taste was special. Their asses was tight to fuck, but it was the taste that I couldn't leave alone. I kept wanting more.

They done their best, sucking and fucking and rimming and doing everything I said. I guess they figured that when I had corned enough, I would let them go. After while there wasn't nothing much left to pump out of me so I got a different idea. I had read about mountain oysters being a favorite in the old west, from animals not boys, and that's where my different idea was special. I gagged them, slit open their nut sacks and watched their pain when I took out what I wanted and turned up the fire on the stove.

Then I sliced off an inch of each of them and they bled more than I figured, they hadn't bled that much when I opened them. I melted some plumbum real quick and used it to staunch the blood flow. They passed out and didn't come to until after I was finished. Then I bound their elbows behind their backs, tied their ankles and knees, wrapped them with chains and pig iron weights, and took them each into the marsh and watched them sink.

It was real interesting the way they held their breaths so long before blowing one long bubble and a few small ones. I had noticed that girls gave up quicker and went ahead and made bubbles and got it over with. I went through their packs. They didn't have much. I tied the packs closed and sank them a few feet from their bodies.

That day I added something new and different to my coastal kills. I got excited all over again just thinking about it on my way back to Charleston. I still do.

Like I said before, there was always a lot of people hanging around my house, no matter whether I was living in Sumter or Prospect or North Charleston and I reckon the reasons people hung around was as different as the people.

Jessie Ruth used to visit my house in Sumter a lot, so did James Judy. Fact is, I introduced them and I was right pleased when they got married. And they kept coming round during the time they lived together after their wedding. That was in North Charleston after I moved back there and was living on Calvert Street. And it was at that same house of mine that Jessie Ruth and James Judy met Johnny Sellers. James and Johnny both was in some deals with me and Johnny moved into James and Jessie's house and rented a room from them. Then James got out of control with drugs so him and Jessie Ruth busted up, but by then Jessie Ruth and Johnny had tasted of each other and liked the flavors so they moved to a different place and started living together.

I kept on doing deals with James Judy and with Johnny Sellers, but I kept my deals with them separate much as I could. Them two didn't see balls to balls about nothing. I've found that some women are contented to let their men do the dealing and them just hang around the edges, not really part of things, but Jessie Ruth weren't one of them kind of women. True she was quiet, kind of shy, but she was right smack in the middle of almost every deal I done with Johnny Sellers just like she had been in on the deals I done with James Judy.

Of course, the thing I liked most about Jessie Ruth was her real great respect for me. Either that or she was scared shitless of me. I never quite figured which. I just know that whenever I said anything she agreed with me and whenever I asked her to do something she usually did it. Without going plumb around my knees to wipe my ass, I'll get to the point. Johnny Sellers was plain dishonest. And that was a drawback. I know that the way the law seen things, everybody in my line of work was dishonest, but we had our rules and wasn't never supposed to be dishonest with them that we done our deals with.

By the way, Johnny was the one that brought Doreen and Robin Michelle to my house in Prospect and left them there and said he couldn't take them back to Charleston because he had to go to Columbia, but I knowed better. Johnny was just plain tired of having Doreen and Robin staying at his house with him and Jessie Ruth and wanted to palm them onto me and my wife. I mention all this here as a reminder of when Johnny's name come up before and to say again he was one son of a bitch who flat couldn't be trusted. Now don't get me wrong, Johnny never fucked up the jobs he done. He was the best and fastest car and boat and truck booster, hot wirer, I ever saw. But Johnny had to be watched real close when it come to the money. Given half a chance, he would walk away with more than his share every time, which leads me straight to the night I murdered Jessie Ruth and him.

Johnny owed me just over a thousand for strip parts he had got from me and sold but never paid me for. After I give that situation some thought, I come up with a way to get him to pay me back. At Picquet Roofing I worked with a man who owned a real nice ocean going fishing boat, outboard motor, and trailer. One Friday noon I overheard him saying he was going to visit relatives and coming back Sunday morning. So Friday night me and Johnny went to that man's house and hooked his boat-n-trailer to Johnny's pickup and hauled it away.

We decided that the best man to fence the boat was Belton Eaddy who lived at Johnsonville near Prospect and specialized in boats and motorcycles. We had done lots of business with Belton before and I knew that he banked Johnny's share on some deals in his cement floor safe.

That night I followed Johnny and Jessie and the boat to Belton's place. We got there pretty late. When I went in, Belton wasn't real happy to see me. He said the law had been watching him and he was planning to quit dealing stole property. I said I had come a damned long way to deliver a boat and I was tired so not to fuck price with me. He went to his bedroom and got the money we agreed was fair. When he come back to the kitchen, he asked me how much for me and how much for Johnny. I took it all and said I would settle up with Johnny later. Then I told Belton that I wanted Jessie Ruth to stay with him a few minutes so I could talk to Johnny alone about a deal. Belton said okay.

I went outside and me and Johnny unhitched the trailer and I told Jessie Ruth to go in the kitchen and wait. I said that me and Johnny would be back in just a little while. She didn't argue. I had told Johnny I knew a house where the owner kept a lot of money and I needed him to go with me to get a look at the layout so we could talk about the best way to topple it one night soon. Johnny said fine and we drove in my car to the Prospect back trail I liked best. Once we was off the highway, I stopped and drew my pistol and ordered Johnny out of the car. He thought I was kidding then knew I weren't.

I made him give me the thirty-eight he carried and I opened the car trunk and took out my thirty-thirty rifle. Johnny knowed what I was going to do and he said he thought we could work things out and I said I didn't think so, he had fucked me out of a lot of money and I was going to get his bank from Belton to repay me. Johnny said I could have his bank, all of it. But I said that wouldn't work because as soon as we got back to Charleston and he was free and loose, he would come after me and kill me. And I would have to be crazy and stupid to allow that.

Johnny smiled at me and said yeah, he understood, then all of a sudden, quick as a jack rabbit, he took off running into the woods. I raised the thirty-thirty and brought him down with one shot to the back of his head. I didn't have to walk to him to see if he was dead. I knew. I left him laying there and went back to the car and drove to Belton's house.

Soon as I walked in, I had the feeling that Jessie Ruth knew I had killed Johnny. She didn't say nothing. I told her Johnny was waiting for us to come pick him up. She walked out to the car and I told Belton we would be back in a few minutes to get the truck. I drove with Jessie Ruth to the same spot where I had took Johnny. I told her to get out of the car then I took the toothpick out of its zipper case under the seat, and I got out.

I said, "you know what I done, don't you?"

She said, "yeah, I know."

I said, "then you understand that I got to kill you, Jessie Ruth. There ain't no other way."

She didn't say nothing back to me. We just walked along a little farther and I swung my arm and drove the knife into her back and she fell forward. I truly don't think she suffered, she was probably dead before she hit the ground. And there I was again, out in the middle of no fucking where digging a grave to bury two more bodies. It seemed like digging and burying was becoming my mainest occupation. Next time I apply for a job, on the application where it says skills, I think I ought to write auto mechanic, roofer, sheet metal worker, killer, grave digger and burier.

When I finished covering the grave, I went back to Belton's house and told him to give me the rest of Johnny's bank and he said, "what am I going to say when Johnny asks for it?"

I said, "Johnny ain't ever going to ask for it." Belton gave me the money.

A few days later I went back to Belton's and got Johnny's truck and took it to Charleston and repainted it and sent it out of state.

When the bodies of Jessie Ruth and Johnny was eventually dug up, the law weren't content just to charge me. Because Jessie Ruth Judy was his legal wife, the law leaned heavy on James Judy and charged him with the murder right along with me. They even threatened him with the death penalty. They said jealousy was the motive, that James Judy had got me to kill Johnny and Jessie

Ruth because Johnny had took Jessie Ruth away from him.

That was a pure and simple bullshit frame. James Judy weren't anywhere near when I killed them two, and he didn't know nothing about it. Still, he had to plea bargain a deal that got him sentenced to ten years, besides which they made him swear to all kinds of lies about him and me which didn't have any truth in them at all.

I killed Jessie Ruth and Johnny just like I said for the reasons that I have said. The rest is crap that the prosecutor dreamed up. It's what I call justice shit, meant to stink up the truth so bad nobody will want to come near it so the law can have things their way.

Likewise, the law went after Belton Eaddy and scared the shit out of him, threatening to charge him with murder if he didn't bargain a plea. He pleaded guilty to accessory after the fact, which was likewise a load of shit. Old Belton didn't know nothing about nothing that happened that night.

There was questions when I got back to Charleston. Jessie Ruth's mama, who didn't like me anyhow, went around saying that Jessie Ruth and Johnny was fearful of Pee Wee Gaskins and in most likelihood I had killed them. I said that that was just a load of bitch shit. And when Johnny's wife, Minnie, asked me if I knowed where her husband and Jessie Ruth was, I said I hadn't seen them in a while. I know she didn't believe me, but at least she had enough gumption to go on about her business and not bother me with more questions.

I put the word out in North Charleston that I wasn't real happy being talked about so reckless and I damn well better not hear about anybody saying anything to the law about me. I let it be known that I specially didn't like bitch shit on my face. The onliest person I went and talked to was James Judy. And I damn sure didn't tell him the truth. I told him that Jessie Ruth and Johnny had gone to live out west somewhere and I doubted they would ever be back.

Horace Jones was a horse's ass, even if he did come recommended real high by the guys I knew in CCI who sent me stole cars. Fact is, the first time I met Horace he had just brought a car to me and left it at the K-Mart parking lot and come to ask me to help him set up a con he run on old folks. I didn't do that kind of shit, but because Horace was sent by nicknames, it were proper for me to be nice to him. I let him stay at our house for a week, and I introduced him to everybody who came to visit me, and I took him around and showed him where things was in Charleston.

He was a presentable man. Some women seemed to think he was handsome. He always wore a suit and tie, like he was going to church or something, and he talked real fancy and liked to use long words. He said he went to college near where he was raised in Alabama and he had learned English literature there, but he never explained to me how that had ever helped him make a living. What I think it did do was make him believe that the world owed him a living. I got the feeling he didn't take real strong to the idea of actually working and that was why he conned old ladies.

He had done time twice, three to five each one. State time for larceny after trust, and federal time for cashing stole social security checks. He looked a mite older than what he said, which was forty. He hadn't long been back in the streets. When he was still at our house after ten days, I reckoned it was time to talk to him about finding a new place to live. But then I got a call and had to make a quick trip to Florence to pick up some good items stole from a doctor's house, and I was gone three days.

When I got back, my wife told me Horace had tried to get between her legs and when she fought him off he turned his dick toward two friends who was visiting her. That pissed me off. Not so much him trying to fuck my wife, but the way he went about doing it. I mean if he had come straight to me like a man and asked to make a deal with me for my wife, I would probably have give her to him for a night or a week or to keep, if the offer were good enough.

But he didn't know what trade meant. He didn't even have a nickname, and never would have one. My problem at that moment was, if I just beat shit out of him and threw him out, I would offend the nickname who had recommended him to me, who was, Horace said, his brother-in-law. Things like that are important. I didn't want to fuck up any of my nickname connections made at CCI. After giving the matter some thought, I decided the solution was really pretty simple. Horace had to die.

Next day I drove to my second choice trail near The Neck to find a spot to dig a hole. Then I went back to North Charleston and told Horace that while I was on my trip I had suddenly remembered these two old maid sister ladies who lived near Johnsonville and I thought they would be just ripe for him to pull his con on. He was real pleased that I weren't mad because he had tried to fuck my wife and that I was going to help him set up his con.

All the way to Prospect I talked to him about these two old ladies I made up in my head from my ideas of what Horace liked and I added in that I thought the inherited money from their daddy and that they was friends of my Mama and I could take him by to meet them in the late afternoon and we would probably both get invited for supper, but I would make my excuses and leave Horace with them to start his con.

Of course, there weren't no old ladies and I didn't have no intentions of doing any of them things I had said. Instead, I drove off the highway and stopped less than twenty feet from the grave I had dug and I drew my Beretta and told Horace to get out of the car.

He tried to act like he weren't scared. He smiled and scraped and said he didn't understand, but I wasn't in no mood for his bullshit. I made him walk straight to the grave and sit down in it. He complained it would ruin his suit and I said he really didn't need to worry about how he was dressed. Then I shot him twice and he fell hack in the grave and I walked over and blew a hole in his head, to make sure he was dead. Then I went through his pockets.

I kept his two hundred dollars, but I buried his wallet, watch, ring and address book a few hundred feet from where I buried him. At my house in North Charleston, I packed his suitcases and told my wife that Horace was taking a bus to New York. She didn't pay much attention. She was just happy he was gone as was most everybody else who bothered to say anything about his absence.

Later I telephoned my ex-CCI friend who recommended him. I said Horace had left for New York with an older lady. I kept his bags in my trunk and sank them with my next coastal kill. I never heard anything else about him.

By late Fall of '74, me and my wife was spending most of our time separated, which was all right with me. She had put up with me long as she could, I guess, and I was about ready to give her away anyhow.

We had already gave our son to my daughter to raise with her kids who was near my boy's age. I bought a mobile home and put it close by my daughter's, near Roper's Crossroads. I stayed there about half my time and in North Charleston the other half. In some ways there was lots of turmoil going on in my life but that Christmas with my grandkids was the happiest and peacefullest I can remember.

14

There's no two ways about it, 1975 was my busiest year and my killingest year and, before it was over, my worst year. My coastal kills was about the same as what they had been for the past five years, young and monthly, boys and girls. Only the first one of that year was different enough to be worth telling about. Along with the pains in my bowels, worser headaches had started coming with the bothersomeness. And added to that, I got these strong needs for more tastes, though I couldn't truly say which was the strongest, for a girl or for a boy.

My luck always being real good, when it's good at all, what I got in January was both. They was in a van that had broke down on the side of the highway just south of Georgetown. Two girls and a boy. Hippie types. I stopped and offered to help and in fifteen minutes I had the van running, but I told them that it had a busted water pump and wouldn't run far or long, and I suggested they leave it and go with me to get a new water pump and I would bring them back and put it on for them. I said that if they didn't have the money to buy a pump I would pay for it and they could send me the money someday. They seemed to like the fact I trusted them. Most people like to feel trusted whether they deserve it or not.

One of the girls wanted to stay with the van, but I told them we wouldn't be gone more than thirty minutes and if they locked it everything inside would be safe. They said okay and got in the car with me and, like all teenage kids, they talked all the time.

The boy was from Oregon, which I had figured from the Oregon tags on the van. He had met up with the girls at some kind of youth hotel specially for college aged kids and they decided to travel together. They seemed real nice and bright and the boy was real funny, said funny things, I mean. I enjoyed their company for that few minutes before I pulled off onto one of my trails, stopped, and drew my Beretta, and handcuffed them. I drove a mile farther on the trail into the swamp, then I got them out. The boy tried to run so I had to hit him with the pistol hard enough to stun him but not do no real damage. Then I taped their mouths, stripped them, put their clothes in my car trunk and started enjoying them.

It was more different than I ever had imagined. It was specially interesting to see how they acted when I made them do things to each other and when I was burning and slicing and opening then closing with plumbum. It was hard to say which one suffered most, I tried to make it equal. In the end, I sank them all together, right next to each other.

But my mainest reason for telling about this here particular coastal kill weren't just because it was the onliest time I ever had two girls and a boy together, it's because after it was over with I had a real serious problem on my hands. The van. It was sure to get found, which was sure to bring the law who was sure to ask questions all up and down the highway. It didn't seem likely anybody seen me or nothing like that, but the law has ways of putting names to owners of vans and contacting next of kin who push investigations which can lead in all kinds of unwanted directions.

I was sure my wise men would say that a van was as bad as a corpse, maybe worse, when it come to evidence. I thought about burning the van, but decided that wouldn't solve nothing, it might even make things worse. Sinking it was out, I couldn't get it far enough out into the swamps for it to sink deep enough not to be spotted. I had to come up with a better way. And I did.

I drove back to the van, took out all the bags, and clothes, and personal things and put them in my car trunk. I didn't even go through their shit. Then

I went back to where I had sank their three bodies and I weighted down and sank their stuff at the same spot. Then I drove straight to my house in North Charleston to get Walter Neely.

Walter Neely. I wish to hell I could tell *Final Truth* without so much as saying his name, but that's impossible. He become the majorist part of my story before it ended so I might as well go ahead and start explaining.

Me and Walter met in CCI where we both done time together. Walter weren't the brightest man I ever met, but it's honest to say that he was a friend, loyal to me. I was his Powerman. Anything I asked, Walter did. And in return I done favors for Walter to make things inside easier for him. After we both was back in the streets, I saw Walter a lot, especially after I moved to Charleston which is where him and his wife, Diane Bellamy Neely, lived.

He stayed at my house in Charleston a lot after him and Diane busted up. Her leaving him nearabout destroyed Walter. He was so upset that nothing seemed to take his mind off how hurt he was, specially when she started seeing Avery Howard who was a real shit ass we both had knowed in CCI and neither one of us trusted or liked worth a damn.

I tried to take Walter's mind off his problem by getting him to take my wife away on trips to places she wanted to go but I didn't. That was about the time me and her had started staying apart a lot more than together. During all the years, from when we was in CCI until he made his wrong turn on me, Walter was a man I trusted as much as I ever trusted anybody. We both had childhoods a lot alike. We used to talk about that from time to time.

Anyhow, to get back to my story, Walter was at my house in Charleston when I got there that evening. I told him that I had been driving up from Beaufort and had seen this van parked in the edge of the woods just off the highway and stopped to check it out and found the keys in it but nobody around so I took the keys and figured we should go back and get it and bring it to the garage for a rebuild and repaint. Walter never questioned my story. He was like that, whatever I said he took without no questions which was good because I never had told him or nobody about coastal kills, and I weren't about to start by telling him what happened to them kids in the van.

We drove out and picked it up and he followed me in it to the garage where over the next few weeks we redone it, painted it black with silver pinstripes, put mag wheels on it, changed the interior, stole a set of dealer tags for it and sent it out of state to sell. When the money come from its sale, I gave a third to Walter instead of his usual twenty percent. He was real happy about that, almost as happy as he had been when I started paying him a hundred dollars apiece to drive stole cars up to Prospect and hide them in different places around there for me.

Sometimes I even took Walter up to Roper's Crossroads for a weekend. He enjoyed my grandkids much as I did. He missed his own kids a lot, I could tell. And when we was in that area, we usually hit Sam's Club, which weren't but a few miles from my trailer, and was my favoritest Club of all. I was a regular there. Everybody knowed me. Fact is, Sam's Club is where I got first-whiff of that murder for money offer that led to lots of things, good and bad.

I knowed John William Powell by sight, but that was all. We hadn't never done no deals and we sure wasn't friends. Then one night he come up to me in Sam's Club and said he knew my reputation from CCI and in the streets, and he wanted to talk to me in the parking lot outside. I had my Beretta in my ankle holster, so I wasn't afraid to walk out there with him. Once we were alone, he said he was looking for a man to kill somebody for a friend of a friend of his.

I got most of these background facts later on from Suzanne and, of course, from what come out at the trial, though a lot of what come out at the trial amounted to pure bullshit. Seems there was this fellow named Silas Barnwell Yates who was a well off landowner about forty-five years old who had a hot thing for a young woman named Suzanne Kipper who I did not know because she come from a different layer than me.

Yates had give Suzanne one of them fancy 260Z sports cars and two saddle horses and lots of other things, and set her up in a mobile home where he used to come stay with her. Just how much of this his wife and family knew about, I couldn't say because I don' t know and frankly I didn't give a shit about his family. I was just interested in him and Suzanne.

Anyhow, the way I heard it, one day Barnwell Yates took the 260Z away from Suzanne then had deputies sent with claiming delivery papers to take the horses and other stuff and throw her out of that mobile home on her ass. That, needless to say, didn't sit real well with Miss Suzanne Kipper. According to what John Powell told me, she went to see a friend of hers named John Owens and said she wanted Owens to help her find somebody to kill Yates. She was serious and willing to pay a thousand dollars. Owens talked to Powell and Powell come looking for me at Sam's Club. I listened to what he said, got his phone number, and said I would think about it and call him soon.

I checked things out through people I knew and found the story was mostly true. I drove past the mobile home where Yates had stayed since him and Suzanne parted company. It was out to itself, with no neighbors around. Three things led me to deciding to do it. First was the challenge of working out a plan, which I always enjoyed doing. Second was that a thousand or more dollars was damned good extra income. And third was concluding that Silas Barnwell Yates deserved killing for the way he had treated that young woman.

I knowed that the hardest part would be getting him out of his mobile home, which needed to be done because I had been well taught by my Wise Friends that indoor crime scenes leave too much evidence. I needed to get Yates out in the woods to kill him and bury him at the same spot. I picked a perfect place for his murder and his grave then I called Powell and had him bring Owens to meet me at a country store. They followed me and I showed them the spot I had chose and we set a time three days later to meet there. They was to bring flashlights, picks and shovels.

And I asked them to bring Suzanne with them. I figured that since she was paying for the job, she had a right to see that it was did proper. Owens said he doubted she would come. I said whether she come or not, she had better send the money. And I wanted five-hundred more than what she had offered. Owens said okay.

The next evening, I drove to Charleston to see Diane Neely who was still Walter's wife but had left his ass because she said he was too mean to her. Diane was a fairly good looking woman with a pretty nice body considering she was twenty nine and had kids. I knew that Avery Howard, the asshole she lived with, was away for a few days, and since Diane was always looking for a way to make a few dollars, like everybody else is, I asked her to follow me up to Prospect in one of my cars and be my bait to get Yates out of his mobile home. I promised her there wouldn't be no trouble. She said okay.

On February 13th, or the night of the 12th, depends on how you look at it, me and Diane drove to a spot about fifty yards from Yates's place and she got out and walked to his front door and knocked. It was real late and she got him out of bed. She said she was having car trouble, could he help her?

It was cold weather and Diane weren't wearing nothing but blue jeans and a real flimsy blouse and no brassiere. Even in dim light it was easy to see her tittie nipples was hard. Silas Barnwell Yates said he would be glad to help her, but I venture he had in mind to work on more than her automobile.

I was waiting crouched behind the car when him and her walked to it. L jumped out and grabbed his jacket collar and shoved the Beretta against his nose and told him to stay quiet or I'd blow him a new nostril. Diane handcuffed his wrists behind his back. I put duct tape over his mouth and shoved him in the trunk.

I drove to where we had left the other car. Diane got in it and went back home, her part was over with. I drove to meet Owens and Powell. I left Yates in the trunk until Owens gave me all of my fifteen-hundred dollars. Then I opened the trunk and told them to take Yates out and drag him to the spot where I planned to bury him.

I got my toothpick and followed. When I pulled off the duct tape he started yelling and screaming and crying and begging and cussing and I don't know what all. He was just plain making too much noise so I hit him hard as I could, right in the adam's apple, to smash his windpipe.

That shut him up and he fell to his knees, but it didn't damage him near as bad as I thought it would so I rammed the toothpick into his chest. It went clear through, but must have missed his heart because he didn't fall over dead when I pulled it out, so I walked around behind him and tilted his head backwards and cut his throat. Then I knew he was dead.

Owens and Powell just stood there in the car headlights, staring at me and the body. After a minute or so, they turned like they was going to leave. I said, "wait a fucking minute, boys. My price don't include nothing but killing. That's the grave spot right next to where he's laying so get busy digging and burying."

I sat down and wiped the knife blade on some grass and put my Beretta on the ground next to me and watched them dig a deep hole, drop Yates in, and cover him up. I drove back to Charleston that night. Next morning, I went by Diane's place and gave her three hundred dollars and told her to forget everything she seen or heard the night before. She said, "I went to a moving picture show last night. I ain't been out of Charleston since before Christmas. She smiled at me, and I knew everything was okay."

Howsomever, a few days later I started doing some serious thinking and worrying. It troubled me to realize that if I had took a harder and closer look at my plan before I done it I would've seen I was making a awful big mistake by allowing two people I didn't even know, much less trust, to eye witness me doing a killing. Never mind that Owens and Powell was as involved and guilty as I was, and for that reason would best keep their mouths shut, I had still broke my own rule of always doing murder alone, including the burying.

Then I commenced wondering something else. Why hadn't that Suzanne Kipper woman come to meet me herself? She didn't have to watch Yates die if she didn't want to. That was okay. But I had this feeling she just didn't want nothing to do with me even though the killing was her idea. But then maybe Powell and Owens hadn't even told her who I was. Maybe they had took all the credit and got more money from her than they give me. I decided right then and there that I badly needed to go have a person to person talk with Suzanne Kipper.

I drove to Lake City, to Sam's Club. There weren't many people around in mid-afternoon, but I got some answers and some news. Suzanne Kipper and John Owens had got married. I also found out where Suzanne Kipper Owens worked and what kind of car she drove. I parked next to her car and when she walked to it, I knew that there was a woman that I had to have. She was beautiful, tall and lean with the longest legs I ever seen on a woman. I swear they run all the way up to her arm pits.

Just as she was opening her car door, I walked up beside her and told her my name was Pee Wee Gaskins. She looked at me and turned white as cow milk. I asked her if she had ever heard of me and she nodded yes and I told her I wanted to sit in her car with her and talk to her. I said that I thought she owed me a few minutes of her time and what I had to say was important to her future and her health.

We got in and I sat on the front seat beside her and I told her that I was happy I had been able to oblige her in the matter of Mister Silas Barnwell Yates and I could definitely assure her he was truly dead. Then I congratulated her on her marriage and took hold of her hand and told her I had something very important to say to her and I wanted her to listen to me real careful.

Her eyes, which was real big and black and beautiful, got even bigger and beautifuller. I said, "in case your new husband didn't give you the details, I sliced your lover boy Yates's throat and I won't hesitate a damn second to do the same thing to you if I ever decide I need to."

From that afternoon on, Mrs. Suzanne Kipper Owens belonged to me. She said her marriage to Owens was at his insistence and a marriage of convenience. I told her I didn't give a flying fuck about that, all I wanted was a taste of her anytime the notion struck me, that I didn't have no reason to hurt her and I wouldn't hurt her so long as she played love fuck with me anytime I wanted, any place I wanted, any way I wanted.

It turned out she was as pretty and tempting naked as I had imagined. That was the most beautiful face and body I had ever touched and tasted, except maybe some of those young and tender coastal kills, but they was just for pleasuring before killing, not sweet love fucking like Suzanne was. We were together lots, anytime I wanted. And the more I was with her, the more I liked her. She was real smart, intelligent, and educated. I could tell she was always trying to figure out what I liked to talk about.

I told her a lot, not just about my life and crimes, though that seemed to interest her, but also about life in CCI and my federal time and the wise men from Elizabeth Street. But even when she relaxed with me, even when we was laughing together, I could feel her fear. She was the one who told me that whenever I comed she felt and smelled and tasted violence and death in it. Knowing that underneath it all she was scared shitless of me was all right with me. I didn't care how she truly felt, just so long as she did everything I asked her to and behaved like the beautiful mistress I wanted her to be.

If I called to tell her to meet me and her husband answered, I told him to drive her to see me and he didn't have no choice but to do it and wait and watch. Of course, later on when John Owens finally got his chance to do in Suzanne and me, he done a real good job, I'll give him that.

Right now, these words of my final truth are about the killing of Silas Barnwell Yates and how I got me one fine woman. As for how this compares with what me and others said later and why, I'll go more into that later on in my story. At that time, I was riding high, and I'm not just talking about riding Suzanne. Deals kept coming to me. Almost every day somebody wanted something from me and give me something in return. There was stories in the newspaper about a prominent Turbeville farmer and businessman Silas Barnwell Yates disappearing, but nobody ever come asking me about him. Suzanne said the law had been to see her because the sheriff knew about her and Yates being lovers and busting up and all that, but the law figured he had just run off with some new young piece and would be back when he was ready.

As for Owens and Powell, the law hadn't even been to see them, like they wasn't suspicioned at all. I even started thinking seriously about marrying another girl I had met. The future couldn't have looked no brighter. Then one evening after everybody had left a party at my house in Charleston, Diane Bellamy Neely showed up and gave me no choice but to do two more serious murders.

I made mention before that I knowed the fellow Diane Neely went to live with after she left Walter. His name was Avery Howard and more than once in CCI he got out of line with me, and other nicknames, and we was forced to have his ass kicked. When I met up with him again on the streets outside, he had already had a couple of bad run ins with Walter, which made it that much worser a situation when Diane left Walter and started living with Avery.

More than once, Avery come to me with a deal, but I turned him down. I didn't want no trade or truck with the bastard. I knew he would stand his own mama on her head just to watch her piss up.

I liked Diane, mainly because I had come to know her real good while she was Walter's wife and I always figured her for smart enough to keep things to herself. But I was wrong again, which I found out when she come to my house that April night. She said that one evening when she and Avery had been drinking a lot and was in bed together she told him about going with me to be my bait to get some man out of his mobile home and that when she seen Yates's picture in the paper and on the television as missing she told Avery that Yates was the man. Then she told Avery about the money I had give her for what she done and he got real mad and said that Yates was a rich man and I had probably stole a lot of money from him and killed him and that what I had give Diane wasn't hog shit. And he told Diane to come see me and tell me that her and Avery wanted five thousand dollars or they was going to drop a dime on me to the law.

When she told me all that, I got so damn mad inside I could have shit fire, but I stayed real calm and even gave Diane a hug and said that come to think of it, Avery was right, they did deserve more, and five thousand sounded fair. Problem was, I said, I kept all my money hid up near Prospect, so I needed to meet them there to do our settling up.

We made plans to meet at an intersection near Lake City the next night at eleven. I asked her to keep Avery from telling anybody and she said she could keep him quiet with the promise of five thousand, which I knew was true because besides being stupid Avery was a greedy bastard.

Next afternoon I drove to Florence, then out to that trail near Prospect where I had buried the others and I dug a grave deep enough to stack two. Then I drove to my trailer at Roper's Crossroads and took a shower and dressed up and went to Sam's Club. I wanted people to see me there. And about eleven o'clock, when the Club was its crowdedest, I slipped out.

Sure enough, Diane and Avery were waiting at the highway intersection. I got in the back seat of their car and gave Avery directions to Prospect and to the turn off onto the trail. I had brought along a lantern type flashlight and a pint of bourbon, which I knowed they was partial to. I passed it around and pretended I was drinking, too. I talked big about how I kept my money out here near Alligator Landing where it was safer than in any bank. I told Avery where to stop and I got out and told them to come with me to get the money because I specially wanted them to see the tree I had hollowed out and put a fire proof safe into.

When a man smells money or pussy, he loses all his common sense, but I think the onliest time a woman loses hers is when she smells money. Whatever the reason, Diane and Avery didn't seem to think there was nothing strange about me having a safe in a hollow tree in the middle of a swamp so they got out of the car and followed right behind me down the path to their grave.

By the time we got there and I shined the light on the fresh-dug ground, it was too late for them. I stepped back behind Avery, put the muzzle of my Beretta to the back of his head, squeezed off two shots, and he fell into the hole. Diane started to run, but I grabbed her, held her around the waist, put the gun against her head and l fired. Then I dropped her on top of Avery.

I had left a shovel near the grave. I put the flashlight and pistol on the ground and spent the next half hour shoveling dirt. There's not really anything more to tell about them. They asked me for what they had coming to them and so I give it to them. Then I drove Avery's car to my Charleston garage, stripped it, and repainted it. By the time Walter got back to town from his trip up to Pennsylvania, Avery's car was out of state and sold.

15

The summer of '75 was real hot. I had a room air conditioner in my trailer near Roper's Crossroads and it did a fine job of cooling things down even when me and my Suzanne was making the whole place rock. And I had a unit just like it, stole from the same store, in my house in Charleston, but it never was enough to cool the whole place so I put it in the bedroom and moved the television in there too and it was fine for me and my new wife. We had got the license in June and was married in the town of Hemingway. She was wife number six and she was eighteen.

Excepting for one nosy old fart, we got along fine with all our neighbors. I was particularly partial to the kids who come to our house a lot and seemed to like me. Sometimes me and Walter and my wife and one or two others would invite a whole passle of boys and girls to go out to the beach and swim and cook hot dogs or we would fix hamburgers on the grill in the backyard.

Kim Ghelkins were a sweet thing, like a combination of a little girl and a young woman, both at the same time. It started off innocent. She went to the beach with us when we took other kids, and she come to our house, into the bedroom, and sat on the bed and watched television where it was nice and cool. I don't think nobody suspected anything when she come there and nobody else was home but me and there weren't no cause for suspicions because I weren't doing nothing to her. But the more I looked at her lying across the bed watching the television, the more interested I become.

After a few weeks I managed to get her to lie down next to me and I cuddled her and touched her little titties. Then later she let me take off her blouse and suck them. I told her that what we was doing was our secret and to promise not to tell nobody. She promised.

Before long I got her to take off her clothes and let me smell and taste of her hardly haired opening. But when I took out my hard dick and asked her to touch it she said no and that she had to leave and she put her clothes back on. I stayed real calm and zipped myself back up and told her I was sorry and I wouldn't do that no more, but Kim still left and didn't come around for a while, and when she did, it was only if other people, specially my new wife, was there too so I couldn't touch or taste her or do nothing, which got to be awful frustrating.

Then when summer was winding down, near Labor Day and school starting and all that, I bought a lot of McDonald's burgers and had a kind of party for the neighborhood kids, including Kim. All the kids called me Uncle Pee Wee, and I went out of my way to be sweet to Kim, which she seemed to like. Then I told her that I was going up to Sumter for that weekend to see my daughter and grandkids and I sure would like to have her go with me and that there would be lots of folks around and I whispered in her ear that I promised to keep my zipper zipped. And I acted ashamed and laughed and teased, and she giggled. After supper was over and all the kids left, Kim left, too, and I figured to myself that that was probably the end of that.

But when I got home from a business deal next afternoon she was waiting in the bedroom with a little overnight bag and said she was ready to go. She just wanted me to promise that she could stay at my daughter's house with all of my grandkids and that I wouldn't try to do any of those things to her again. I promised. And I didn't ask if she had asked her folks if she could go with me. Whether she had or hadn't didn't really matter.

It was almost dark when we got to my mobile home at Roper's Crossroads. I knowed my daughter and her husband and their kids had gone away for the weekend so when we went in my trailer, I told Kim that probably everybody was at the grocery store buying food for the weekend and would be back shortly. And I busied myself with turning on the air conditioning and opening two soft drinks and putting away some snacks I had stopped and bought.

Then I went in the bathroom and took a shower and came out naked and grabbed Kim before she could get out of the chair she was sitting in watching television. She weren't strong. I didn't have no trouble holding her face down on the floor and getting her wrists cuffed and picking her up and laying her on the bed. She started crying, "you promised, Uncle Pee Wee!" But I was too busy taking her clothes off to pay much attention to anything she was saying.

When I had her naked I tasted her. Then I spread her open and fucked her cherries, front and back. At that point she felt more love fuck than coastal except that I knew it weren't going to end there. I came once then went out and brought the duffel from the car and got a plastic drop cloth from the pantry and spread it on the floor and laid her on it.

I didn't tape her mouth. I burned and cut and plumbum plugged her then I sliced and carved her and I ran the toothpick deep and twisted it. The sounds of her screams were more pleasuring than I had imagined those times when I hadn't dared take gags off others. When I quit, she was unconscious.

I slept for a while and when I woke up she was whimpering, barely alive, and I started on her again. She was real sweet to live so long. It was like she knew that the longer she waited to die, the more pleasuring she would give her Uncle Pee Wee. I kissed her and I thanked her for the greatest joy I had ever got from any coastal kill or serious murder, but she didn't seem to be listening, like it didn't matter to her, but it was important to me. I choked her to death while I corned again.

I buried Kim that evening near Roper's Crossroads, not on my trail at Prospect. She were different and special. I would have took her to the tenant house and laid her next to Janice, but somebody had bought that place and was living there. Somebody still is.

Needless to say, Kim's family was awfully upset that she disappeared. Her school teacher was upset, too. So was my wife and daughter. Everybody who knew Kim was asking questions. I said that Kim had been supposed to meet me and my wife to go to my daughter's house for the weekend, but she hadn't never showed up at our house, and that when I drove by her house there wasn't nobody at home. That story held up because a neighbor had seen me at mid-day stop and go to the door of Kim's house and get no answer and get in my car and drive away.

Another neighbor had seen Kim leaving the house earlier, long before I got there, so that helped a little to push suspicions away from me. Of course, truth was, my wife had went off somewhere else and didn't know nothing about no weekend trip plans with Kim and neither did my daughter so I didn't reckon they believed me at all.

That's when I decided that me staying in Charleston right then might not be such a good idea. So I told my wife and daughter and Suzanne that I had to go to Florida on a deal for a few weeks. L drove down south of Savannah and rented a tourist cabin to lay low until things calmed down. Based on my experience, I knowed that things always quietened after a while so I didn't think I needed to go real far away or stay gone very long. I certainly didn't believe I had more to worry about than I could handle. Things didn't appear to me to be any seriouser than when Janice and Patty and Peggy had all took missing at once. And I had got through all that without no problems.

What I didn't know was that Kim's school teacher was riding the law's ass to find her, and Kim's daddy was running around playing detective. If I had knowed then what was going to happen, I would've took my fastest and best car and gone straight up to Canada and disappeared forever.

After I had been laying low a while, I went back to Charleston to the garage I rented for working on stole cars where I kept a cot and a change of clothes. I planned on staying there instead of going home and having to answer more questions. But when I got to the garage, I was in for a big surprise. The car and pickup that I had been working on was gone. So was all the parts I had boxed up to deliver with them, plus all my tools. Some son of a bitch had stole everything. And I had a damned good idea who done it. Dennis Bellamy.

Dennis was the brother of Diane Bellamy Neely, Walter's wife who had run off to live with Avery Howard, who I killed with her but nobody knowed at that time that they was dead except me. It was through Diane that I had met Dennis and his, and her, half-brother, Johnny Knight, and we started doing deals together. Dennis was good at boosting parts and he had taught everything he knowed to Johnny who was just fifteen but had been stealing car parts since he was ten when he started out with hubcaps. Now he was damn near good as Dennis, and they worked as a team.

Because they was both good mechanics, I hired them from time to time to help me and Walter at the garage. I was teaching Johnny how to do refinishing, from emerying to priming to coating and lustring, and he was getting good. Him and Dennis both had keys to the garage; and I reckoned that they had decided that since I wasn't around they would just help theyselves to whatever they wanted. Of course, I wasn't about to go looking for Dennis and Johnny in them clubs and tonks because I didn't want to be seen myself so I decided it would be a good idea to find out what Walter Neely might have heard or knew.

I called him and he met me at a store near Mount Pleasant, a little town outside Charleston on the way to Sullivan's Island and Isle of Palms. I told Walter about all my stuff being stole and asked if he knowed what was going on and he said he had seen Dennis and Johnny driving the pickup that had been in my garage and which we had just changed from blue to red, and he figured the car we had been working on was probably at Dennis' house, too, along with all my tools.

    I told Walter to find Dennis and tell him I weren't mad, I just wanted my truck and car and spare parts and tools brought back. Then I told Walter to be home next evening and I would telephone him to find out what Dennis said.

    I drove to Roper's Crossroads that night and parked a half mile from my trailer and snucked through the woods to it. There weren't nobody around so I went inside. Then I walked to my daughter's and woke her and asked her if the law had been around and she said they hadn't, but there had been a man looking for me who said he was Kim's Daddy and my daughter had told him I was out of town, which I was. I stayed at my trailer and nobody come there looking for me. It seemed like, sure enough, things was calming down.

    Next night I called Walter who had found Dennis who said that he had heard talk that the law was asking lots of questions about me and he had been afraid that sooner or later they might find my garage so him and Johnny had cleaned everything out of there and was holding it for me and would bring it to me wherever I said, whenever I said.

    I asked Walter how much stock he took in that story, and Walter said he thought it was a load of bullshit. He figured that Dennis and Johnny had stole my stuff and hid it and planned to wait and see what happened. If it turned out I was in deep shit and didn't come back or ended up in jail, they would've sold everything and kept the money for theirselves.

    I agreed with Walter that he was right though I knowed that Walter flat hated Dennis Bellamy and I didn't believe much he ever said against Dennis because Walter blamed Dennis for turning his sister, Diane, against Walter. Walter never could admit that his beating Diane was the real reason for her splitting with him. I reckoned that the onliest person Walter hated more than Dennis was Avery Howard who he thought had stole Diane from him. I guess it could be said that Walter didn't see things too awfully straight.

I told Walter to go see Dennis and Johnny and talk real nice to them and tell them to please bring all my things to my trailer at Roper's Crossroads. Walter could drive his pickup and take them back to Charleston. I said to tell them that I figured I owed them, and I surely intended to pay them for taking care of my things.

Next evening when they arrived, Dennis was driving the repainted car. Johnny was driving the stole truck. Walter was leading the way in his pickup. They come inside. I had a case of beer cooling in the fridgerator. We all had one, then I gave Dennis a thousand dollars and Johnny five hundred and I thanked them for going to my garage and taking all my stuff so the law wouldn't find it. We laughed and kidded about it then we walked out to the truck and I looked in back and seen that everything was there. About that time, my daughter and her kids got home and everybody spoke to everybody cause they all had met and knowed each other one time or another there or in Charleston.

After my daughter and her family went on into their mobile home, I told Dennis and Johnny that I was expecting some more questions from the law in Charleston so I planned to spend most of my time in the Sumter and Florence area, but I planned to keep on doing strip and rebuild car deals because I still had my good out of state connections so I needed Dennis and Johnny to continue to help me. And, of course, with all that money I had just give them, they believed me.

I told Walter to offer Johnny some sandwich makings and turn on the television while me and Dennis rode down the road to look at an old barn I planned to fix up for a garage to work in. I said I needed Dennis's opinion about what to do with it. Dennis and me left in my car and drove to the Prospect trail that was my favorite. We got out and Dennis said he didn't see no building and I shined my flashlight into the swamp and said, "look right past that big oak." And in the split second he stared to where I pointed the beam I drew my Beretta and shot him twice in the head.

I wasn't worried that anybody would hear or see, so I got back in my car and drove to my trailer. I told Johnny that Dennis was full up with ideas about the barn and had waited there while I come and got him and Walter so we could all talk more about our plans. I waited a few minutes while Johnny finished his ham sandwich. Then we went out and got in my car and drove to where I had just killed Dennis and, soon as we got out, I shined my flashlight up into a tree and asked Johnny if he thought that tree was strong enough to chain in an engine hoist. And when he stared up at where the beam pointed, I put the muzzle to the back of his head and pulled the trigger and killed him.

Then I looked at Walter in the car headlights. He was nodding his head up and down and I weren't real sure whether he was approving what I done or just wondering if he was next. I shined the flashlight across the clearing to Dennis's body and I said, "I never did like that shit ass."

Walter said, "me neither."

I stood real quiet. This here were a special situation that needed some careful thinking and deciding. First off, I had broke the rule about letting anybody see me do murder, but it was too late to go back and change that. What I needed to know now was whether I could trust Walter to keep quiet about what he just witnessed. I thought the answer to that was yes because Walter and me went back a long ways and all the times I had ever trusted him before he hadn't never let me down.

On the other hand, him witnessing me committing a murder was seriouser than anything I ever trusted him about before then. Still and all, I surely could trust him more than them two, Powell and Owens, who had seen me kill Yates. I didn't even know them. But then them two had been involved with me in killing Yates and that was why I felt sure they would keep quiet.

What I decided to do then was involve Walter to truly test him. To begin the test, I walked to the trunk of my car and took out two shovels and handed one to Walter and asked him to help me dig a grave. He didn't fail me, we commenced digging. When we had got the hole deep enough for two bodies, we stopped and rested, and I figured that right then was the time for the rest of Walter's test. If he passed it, fine. If he didn't, I would just dig this grave deep enough for three.

I took the flashlight and shined it across the clearing to another part of the swamp and I told Walter to look where the beam was pointing, and I said, that's where I buried Diane and Avery. And standing there in that empty grave, with two corpses a few feet away, I told him the story about Diane helping me get Yates out of his house and then her and Avery trying to blackmail me about it, not leaving me no choice but to kill them. When I finished talking, Walter was real quiet, and I asked him if he thought I done the right thing by killing them.

He said, "yes," he thought I done right, that they really hadn't give me no choice, and he was glad Avery was dead, for stealing Diane away from him, like he was glad Dennis was dead, but he felt a little sad about Johnny cause he was a good kid and he couldn't help but feel sad about Diane because he had loved her and they had been married and had kids and all. But now that was all over and done with so he wasn't going to cry. Then he looked at me and said is anybody else I know buried out here?

I said Johnny and Jessie Ruth. He nodded slow again and I knew that he was thinking to hisself that now he had become a after the fact accessory. I didn't say nothing else. I just climbed out of the grave and walked to the two bodies and took my money out of their pockets. Then Walter helped me drag them to the hole. That's when he said he sure did like them new shoes Johnny was wearing, and it seemed a shame to bury them, and did I think it would be all right for him to keep them? I shook my head and smiled inside. Walter had passed the test.

He might be kind of dim, but he was a loyal friend and the least of my worries was that he might ever turn around and roll over on me. So I made another mistake and didn't abide by the Wise Men's rule to never keep anything from a victim because it's evidence. I said sure, take the shoes, and he did, and when we got back to my trailer he took them inside and said he was going to leave them there for a while until it was safe to wear them back to Charleston without no chance of nobody recognizing them.

We sat up most of that night talking. Walter asked me lots of questions and I answered too many of them. He drove back to Charleston next morning. I told him to just go about his business like usual and not tell anybody he had seen me or even been near Sumter. He said he understood. Far as I was concerned, killing Dennis and Johnny was just the easiest way to solve one more business problem. Now all I had to do was go back to Savannah and lay low a while longer. Things was bound to get back to normal soon.

While I was staying near Savannah I kept on coastal killing because I didn't want nothing ever to stop that. And during the same time a whole lot of things was going on around Charleston and Sumter concerning me only I didn't know nothing about what was happening until it was too damn late.

Before October ended, Kim Ghelkins's Daddy had went back to Sumter and got a deputy to go with him to Roper's Crossroads and illegally search my mobile home. Inside they found some of Kim's clothes which she had stuck in the bedroom closet. I reckon that my mind had been so full of thoughts about what I was set on doing to her I hadn't noticed her hanging them there.

That was a major fuckup. True, her clothes didn't prove anything except that sometime or other Kim had been in my trailer, but it convinced her Daddy that I knew more about what had happened to her than I was telling. And when he told the law in Charleston about finding Kim's clothes, they got even more suspicious and commenced looking for me in earnest. And though they couldn't find me, they did find out that several other people I knowed had also been missing for a while so the law started doing some heavy pressing. And the man they pressed hardest was Walter Neely.

To Walter's credit, he held up real well. When they picked him up and questioned him, he didn't admit nothing about nothing. He said he hadn't seen me in almost two months, that he remembered a lot of kids wandering in and out of my house in Charleston, but he didn't know their names and he didn't think I ever done more than just take them swimming or cook hot dogs and burgers for them and be nice to them.

The lawmen couldn't shake Walter. He had been run around that track too many times before. And I'm convinced that they never would've got nowhere with him if I had been someplace where Walter could have talked to me. But when they let him loose after questioning and he tried to find me, nobody could tell Walter where I was because nobody knew and so Walter didn't know which way to turn. And that's when he made the biggest fucking mistake of his life. And mine. He decided to go talk to his preacher.

Meanwhile, the law in Charleston and Sumter was getting real frustrated at not finding me so they got together with the State law and come up with a strategy to corner Pee Wee Gaskins.

They had witness statements that Kim Ghelkins had been at my house at different times and that she had said she was going on a trip with me for the weekend. They had found her clothes, or at least what her Daddy said were her clothes, in my trailer at Roper's Crossroads. And though the law knew that the evidence they had wouldn't support any real serious charges, it was enough for them to take out a felony warrant charging me with contributing to the delinquency of a minor.

They planned to use that warrant to hunt me down and arrest me and put me in jail. And once they had me behind bars, they figured on asking me all the rest of their questions about what happened to Kim, plus also asking me about all them stole cars they had found parked near my trailer.

Sometimes luck shines its light of pure miracles down on me. Other times it just takes a huge shit. The biggest, worse smelling, bad luck turd in my life landed splat on top of me on November 14, 1975.

I had decided the night before that things had probably cooled off enough for me to go back to Roper's Crossroads. I parked a half-mile away, like I done the time before, and went through the woods. And that's when I seen the deputy parked across the road from my daughter's mobile home. I turned around and snucked back to my car and drove straight away to the truck stop near Florence and use one of them outside phones to call Walter collect. He sounded shaky and I got the idea real quick that he thought his phone was tapped. All he would say was, "they was here today. They said they got a warrant for your arrest."

I said, "on what charge?"

But Walter didn't know so I thanked him and told him to take care of hisself, then I hung up and left. I drove to one of them rest stop places and sat there and thought my mind was a minute a mile. What the hell could they have a warrant for? They didn't have no bodies unless Owens or Powell had gone in and confessed, which weren't likely, or Walter had turned which was even less likelier. And there weren't no garage for them to find. But there was them stolen cars parked near my trailer and I figured that was probably what this was all about.

But it didn't really matter what the charges was, I didn't plan on going back to prison for any reason. That's when I suddenly thought about the duffel bag in my car trunk. The things inside it weren't evidence of nothing, but still it didn't seem a good idea to let things like that get found.

I drove backroads to swamps near The Neck and I sank everything in that bag with all the pig iron and chains I had left. I even sank them handcuffs I had been so careful to take care of. Once that was done, I sat there alone in the middle of the Neck wondering where to go and what to do next.

Then I remembered that the car I was driving was registered in my own name. I had titled it when I got my license renewed and there weren't no doubt that if they had took out a warrant for me, they was looking for this car. And since I knew there was a deputy watching my trailer at Roper's Crossroads, I couldn't go there to get another car. And the law was surely watching Walter and my wife and everybody else I knew, too, so I couldn't go to them for help. I searched my mind for what I had learned in federal and I remembered, the bigger the crowd, the harder it is to spot one man.

That had worked for me when I hid out with the carnival and I still had a few contacts in carnivals. Or I could go to New York to Elizabeth Street. And there was also men in other states who I knowed in CCI who I was pretty sure would help me out if I could get to them. That was the problem, how was I going to get to any of them?

I kept on thinking while I broke down my thirty-thirty rifle and put it and my Beretta and the toothpick in my suitcase. I wasn't sure what to do with them things. They was all evidence, but it was hard to part with them, particularly that knife. It was special. In a way it was as much a part of me as my dick, it surely had brought me as much pleasure. And it could kill, which was something I never had been able to do with my dick, no matter how hard I tried.

It took a while but the answers finally come. I drove to Sumter on back roads to a junkyard where I parked and waited until just before daylight. Then I pulled and pushed hoods and fenders and parts around my car and took off the tags and threw them in a scrap heap and, carrying my suitcase, I walked into town. The streets was mostly empty that early in the morning. I hung around an alleyway near the post office until it opened, then I went inside and bought one of them big padded mailing envelopes and went into a toilet booth in the men's rest-room and took the toothpick out of my suitcase and wrapped it in a tee shirt and put it in the envelope and addressed it.

The clerk at the counter obliged me with a stapler to close the padded envelope, then he weighed it and I paid him and he put the postage on it and put it in a mail sack. At least I had managed to get one murder weapon safely hid away. Then I went to a phone booth in the post office and called the bus station and asked the time for buses to Savannah. I figured that was the fastest way out of South Carolina, and from there I could connect to Florida. I was in luck, the bus I wanted was leaving in under an hour. I called a taxi and had it pick me up at the post office. I had enough time to make a couple of stops, to do a few other things.

But I didn't get to go nowhere or do nothing. The law, lots of law, stopped the taxi and dragged me out and laid me face down and searched me and cuffed me and read me my rights and took me to jail and locked me in a cell. That's when they told me I was charged with contributing to the delinquency of a minor and I didn't know whether to laugh or fart. But I didn't do neither. I acted real serious and said I didn't have no idea what they was talking about.

And when they asked me where I had been, I said I had been out of state on business, and I had just got back and heard that they still hadn't found Kim Ghelkins so I had decided I would go to Savannah and look for her because I remembered her once saying she was thinking of running away to live in Savannah.

But this time nobody was buying my story. They acted like Kim's clothes in my trailer was a capital crime all by theyselves. They didn't mention Johnny's shoes cause they didn't know nothing then about any of them killings. They just kept questioning me over and over about Kim and I kept giving them the same old shit answers.

Then they started threatening me with charges of grand theft auto on the cars parked near my trailer at Roper's Crossroads. Fast as they come up with threats and questions, I come up with answers. I swore that them cars was brought to me by boys from Charleston who offered to sell them to me cheap and I had let them leave them at my place until I could check them out and see how they run and decide whether to buy them or not. I offered to give the law the names of who had brought me those cars in exchange for immunity.

The law didn't buy into that one either. And even though they didn't have enough hard evidence to make chicken feathers stick to chicken shit, and they knew it, and they knew I knew it, still they kept on holding me for questioning, and holding me on suspicion, and holding me for contributing to a minor's delinquency.

I thought that at anytime they might bring in the toothpick I had mailed. I figured the post office clerk had recognized me and called the law and would tell them about the package I mailed. But it turned out it wasn't him who called the police, it was a businessman who seen me getting in the taxi. When I had been in jail for almost three weeks, the public defender's office started making big noises about them holding me illegally, and I was thinking that any day, hell any minute, I was going to walk. Then all hell broke loose. Walter Neely turned and I was in the deepest shit of my life.

Much as I hate what that son of a bitch done to me, I don't hold Walter wholly to blame. I just wish there had been some way we could have talked before he went to his preacher. As I said before, up until then Walter had always been a loyal friend to me, and me to him. Sure, he could be mean and rough as a rasp, and he weren't no genius, but that ain't what's important. What is important is that somebody who really didn't give pig shit about Walter got hold of him and ruined a perfectly good man.

The law had kept leaning heavy on Walter and Walter had just stood straight and took it, but when he heard they had me in jail at Sumter, he got so worried he turned panicky. Later I was told he said he started having dreams about me killing Diane and he started feeling real guilty about being there when I killed Dennis and Johnny, and him helping me bury them.

It was told to me that Walter got so scared when he was alone in the dark that he started thinking he seen ghosts and he got specially nervous if anybody ever mentioned the names of any of them people that I had told him I killed. Because of all that was happening to him, Walter went and talked to a preacher about everything. I imagine that preacher had to clean out his drawers first, but then he told Walter they ought to pray and ask for guidance so Walter and the preacher prayed and prayed until finally Walter was ready to make his confession to God and get redeemed and be borned again into the salvation of Jesus Christ. All of which would've been fine if he had just stopped right there, but then the preacher convinced Walter that they also ought to go one step higher and have a talk with the law.

First off, Walter told lawmen about Dennis Bellamy and Johnny Knight, the two killings he witnessed and was involved in. Then he told them that Pee Wee Gaskins had a whole graveyard full of people he had killed. When he told them that two of the bodies was Diane Neely and Avery Howard, them lawmen jumped on Walter and said they was sure Walter was in on committing that murder, too, because they knew Diane was his wife who had run off with Avery.

And later, when Walter said two of the other bodies buried there was Johnny Sellers and Jessie Ruth Judy, them same lawmen went straightaway looking for James Judy because they was sure he must have been in on committing that murder because Jessie Ruth was his wife and Johnny had took her away from him.

When I heard all that horse shit, I decided that them lawmen all had fucking one track minds. Of course, they never would have found any bodies at all, or known any more about my serious murders than they know now about my coastal kills, if it hadn't been for Walter Neely suddenly getting saved, which also got his ass charged with murder. But then I guess the law reckoned that since Walter had been borned again, he wouldn't mind dying in the electric chair.

As it turned out, Walter Neely led lawmen all over Prospect looking for the bodies he said I had buried. Walter didn't have much sense, or much sense of direction either. It took him days to find the right trail then it took lawmen days of digging empty holes before they finally dug up Dennis Bellamy and Johnny Knight on December 4, 1975

Next morning they dug up Johnny Sellers and Jessie Ruth Judy and, that afternoon, Diane Neely and Avery Howard. I was told that Walter got so upset he had to be sedated when he saw them pull what was left of Diane out of the ground. Seems he recognized her clothes. I guess I should've buried her naked. Five days later, on December 10th, Walter managed to lead them to Doreen and Robin Michelle. Suddenly my picture and story was all over the newspapers and television news. Sometimes I think I must've growed myself a four foot dick to be able to bend it around and fuck myself like I done when I trusted Walter Neely.

In the end, it weren't the work of no brilliant lawmen from Sumter or Charleston or the State that brought me down. It was my own doing, letting Walter know where all them bodies was. The wise men of Elizabeth Street was right. If bodies don't get found, killers don't get caught.

But in December of 1975, the coroner had the bodies, and Jesus had Walter, and the law had me.

16

They transferred me to the Florence jail because they found the bodies in Florence County. They held me and Walter both "pending the coroner's inquest" which they finally got around to holding on April 27, 1976. Meantime the law had arrested James Judy and they spent all their time going from me, to Walter, to James, comparing stories and trying to get me to confess to multiple homicides, which I weren't about to do.

The evidence at the inquest was pretty solid. In the end they charged me and Walter with eight counts of murder, and James Judy with one count of murder and one count of accessory to murder. That was my first head on collision with Solicitor T. Kenneth Summerford, and Old Double Barrel was damned determined from the outset he was going to burn my ass. He decided to try me alone just on the charge of killing Dennis Bellamy. He picked that case because of the evidence. In Dennis's head they found two thirty-two bullets that the ballistics lab said come from the Beretta I was carrying when they arrested me.

And the law knowed it was smart to separate my trial from Walter's because Walter would say whatever the law wanted him to say. They even got Walter to tell about Johnny's shoes only they got him to say that I was the one who took them. The law even threatened to prosecute my daughter if she didn't testify against me, specially about them stole cars and seeing me and Walter with Dennis and Johnny the night they was killed.

My trial started May 24, 1976. My only defense was my story of what happened that night. I said that Dennis and Johnny come to visit me with Walter and I had loaned my pistol and car to Walter and the last I seen of them, Johnny and Dennis had left with Walter, who must've took them out and killed them with my pistol and buried them near where he had buried his wife, and her lover, and them others he had killed. Hard as it might be to believe, I truly weren't out to get Walter's ass fried with them lies. I just wanted to make the jury have some reasonable doubts that I had did the murder. I figured that later, at Walter's trial, he could get them to have reasonable doubts about him doing it, too.

But Old Double Barrel wouldn't turn loose. He did a summing up talk to the jury that run the better part of two hours. He beared down hard on the ballistics report and he took everything I had said and tore it to pieces. He said that the reason I had an answer for everything was because ever since I was arrested all I had done was sit in a cell and think up stories that made just enough sense that the jury might believe them. And that's exactly what I had did.

Not to make this whole part of my story too long and boresome. On May 28, five days after the trial started, the jury found me guilty. And circuit judge Dan McEachin sentenced me to death in the electric chair.

My lawyer was Ernest B. Hinnant and, in all fairness, he done as good a job as he could, but between the evidence and Old Double Barrel there was no way I could win. My conviction and death sentence made James Judy decide to plea bargain a deal on his accessory charge in Jessie Ruth's murder. The law claimed that James paid me to kill Jessie Ruth, which was a wagon load of horse shit. As I've already said. James Judy didn't have nothing to do with Jessie Ruth's and Johnny Sellers' killing, or any of the others. He wasn't around and he didn't know nothing about anybody I killed no matter what the prosecutor tried to pressure people to say.

Walter Neely's trial started the week after mine ended. His main defense, his lawyer said, was that he was retarded and under the control of Pee Wee Gaskins. In a way, I reckon that was true, too. Walter surely weren't real bright and he did pretty much anything I asked him up until he got borned again and forgot all about what loyalty and friendship meant. Walter is serving life. That's all. Just one life sentence. I hope the bastard rots.

I had swore I wasn't never going to prison again, but all of a sudden there I was, not just back in CCI, but locked in cell block two on that tier with the special cells they call Death Row.

My lawyer said my appeals would take a few years, but I didn't want to count on appeals. There was seven more indictments for murder hanging over my head. Even if my appeals was successful, which weren't likely, I still had to deal with them other charges. I didn't want to confess to anything I was charged with, but I knew that if I proved to even one lawman that I had knowledge about any crimes that they didn't know anything about, I might be able to put myself in position to cut a deal.

I knowed that lawmen just flat can't stand having unsolved murders in their files and even worser in their minds is to find out about a murder that they didn't even know had been committed. So the first thing I did, to get my plan moving my way, was to tip a Sumter lawman about Patty's body being buried in that septic tank. I never could figure why it took so long, but it was November before the law found the right house and septic tank and Patty.

As it turned out, I shouldn't have done that tip at all because before they found her body and even before I was settled good in my new cell on Death Row, the Supreme Court declared South Carolina's death penalty unconstitutional. I didn't know the legal reasons and I didn't give a farmer's fart.

Suddenly I was off Death Row and back on the yard and tiers of CCI with my reputation powerfuller than ever because now I was a nickname with two murders to his credit and seven more murder indictments hanging over him and I had just walked away from Death Row and an appointment with The Chair.

And because of the television and newspaper publicity about all the bodies dug up at Prospect, I was downright famous. Men come out of their way in the yard to shake my hand or to ask me to pose for pictures with them and their families on visitors days. Even the Warden showed me some respect.

For protection, Walter Neely was doing his life sentence at another prison, but even if I could have got to him, I don't think I would've killed Walter, though I surely did want to talk to him.

Awhile after I was back on the yard, the Sumter and state law come to talk to me about Patty's body which they had finally got identified, but I said I didn't have no idea what they was talking about. I said that any tip they had got about her body being in that septic tank damn sure hadn't come from me.

Of course, that made the lawman I had tipped mad as hell. He called me a damned liar, but it were his word against mine. Then in early December, the Charleston law come with SLED to see me about Barnwell Yates. Because he was a big fart in a small room, lawmen hadn't quit searching for him during them two years. They questioned me and took me from CCI to where Yates's body was found and tried to get me to confess to killing him. They claimed they had found his body after they located Kim Ghelkins's body which they had found after they found Patty in the septic tank. They said all their findings resulted from their search for all the victims of Pee Wee Gaskins.

I told them I appreciated their efforts to shovel all their bullshit unsolved murder charges onto me, but I didn't have no fucking idea what they was talking about and I didn't have nothing more to say. Two days later, the law announced they had dug up Clyde Dicks and right then and there it was obviouser than hell to me that Walter Neely was still doing a lot of talking. There just weren't no way they could have ever knowed to search for bodies in all them different places unless Walter told them.

Every corpse they dug up was one of the ones I had told Walter about when I thought I could trust him that night we buried Johnny and Dennis, when I told him about Diane and Avery because they had tried to blackmail me over Diane luring Yates out of his mobile home so's I could kill him. I told him about most of the ones who was our friends or we had done deals with. He hadn't knowed Clyde, but for some reason I told him about her, too. Then, I recollect thinking that I was talking too damn much, even to Walter, and I shut up, and it was a good thing that I stopped before I said anything about Coastal kills or them other serious murders.

I know now that Walter told the law everything I ever told him and that's the reason he never was charged with nothing else, not even when they come after me with more death penalty charges. And though it was Walter who tipped the law about me killing Barnwell Yates, it was Owens and Powell who really fucked up that situation. When the law questioned them, they both went limp dick and put me and Suzanne in the middle of everything. The way they told it, she was the ring leader and the brains, and I was the hired killer.

We was all four charged in the Yates murder, and the trial was moved from Williamsburg County, which is where Yates was killed, to the town of Newberry, north of Columbia. Even though our defense lawyers wanted separated trials, the Court ruled we could all be tried together.

Our trial was set for April of 1977.

The idea of standing trial with me scared hell out of Suzanne and I didn't blame her. With my reputation for killing, having just got reprieved from The Chair and with seven more murder indictments against me, she was afraid she might be in line for the death penalty herself, which was what the prosecution was telling newspapers and television they was going to seek on all four of us, even though there weren't no such thing as a legal death penalty statute in South Carolina at that time. When we got a chance to talk on the phone, I told her that she should just keep quiet and say nothing. But the prosecutor's pressures and her own fears was just too much for her. She plea bargained and was sentenced to Life.

At the trial I swore I was just the accessory that had lured Yates from his house and turned him over to Owens and Powell who killed and buried him. But them two convinced the jury that Suzanne had hired me and paid me directly and I had done everything else. All they done, they said, was be the go betweens and deliver the money. One more time I got found guilty of murder, and Judge Dan P. Laney sentenced me to life imprisonment. Again.

Owens and Powell are both back out in the streets now. Some life sentences don't last as long as others. Every time Suzanne comes up for parole the whole case gets rehashed in the newspapers and she gets turned down. She figured to serve ten years at the most, but she was still inside after thirteen.

There's one more part to Suzanne's story. I'll tell it later.

17

Having two life sentences added even more weight to my nickname in CCI, but I still made it a special point to keep on my goodest behavior and by the end of the year of 1977 I was pretty much back in charge of things.

When I say in charge I don't mean I thought I ran the whole of CCI. What I mean is that I could get pretty much anything I needed. I had the system working for me or, as we said it inside, I had shit on my dick and blood on my shank. I had my power and my weapon and all the young meat I wanted.

I wished sometimes I had my toothpick instead of a joint made shank, but my shank was easy to keep hid and that toothpick, much as I loved him, was too long to hide anywhere.

They still had me on cell block two, where guards could keep their eyes on me, but I got along fine with them and all the other prison officials. I was always polite and cooperative and gave them no shit that they could recognize by sight or smell. Whatever else I done and got done was inside my system and they never knew nothing about that. I got to the place I was feeling pretty damn sure of myself. Don't get me wrong, I weren't happy pulling double life in CCI, but since that was the way things was, I decided to make the best of it, like I had done before.

Time was on my side. One thing prison teaches you is that you got to be patient. I figured that in a few years I would be able to plan and carry out another one of those escapes for which I was famous. What l didn't know then was that me doing double life sentences weren't enough to satisfy Prosecutor

Summerford. He was just biding his time until he was ready to come after me again.

And he got his chance when the South Carolina Legislature passed a new death penalty law copied after the one in Georgia which the U.S. Supreme Court had ruled in '76 was constitutional. Up until then, Summerford hadn't seemed interested in trying me on any of them seven other murder charges, but once the new death penalty law was put on the books, he couldn't wait.

He come after me for the murder of Johnny Knight, the young guy who I killed with Dennis Bellamy. He had ballistics evidence and he had Walter as a witness, exactly the same as he had had in the Bellamy case, and I reckon he figured he could convict me just like he done then. Old Double Barrel got the indictment true billed in early '78. The trial was set for Florence County in April.

I had two good lawyers, John K. Grisso and Grady Query, but when Prosecutor Summerford announced he was going for the death penalty and jury selection started, I got the feeling they was more nervous than I was. I asked them how it was possible for me to be give the electric chair when the killing I done was before the new death penalty law come into being? And my lawyers said that that was a very good question and also a valid point of law, but unfortunately the matter couldn't be settled until I was convicted and sentenced to be executed and that was appealed all the way to the U.S. Supreme Court. And they thought I could wind up losing just as easy as winning, and if I lost, my ass was ashes.

What my lawyers could do for me, they said, was go talk to Prosecutor Summerford and try to get him not to seek the death penalty by striking some kind of a deal. They talked, and what my lawyers and Old Double Barrel come up with was this. If I pleaded guilty to all seven of them other murders the prosecutor wouldn't ask for the death penalty, and the judge would agree to sentence me to seven consecutive life sentences following the two I already had for Bellamy and Yates.

My lawyers seemed to think that was the best deal they could get. And fair or not, it suited hell out of me because right then I was ready to take all the life sentences they wanted to give me, just so long as they kept me out of The Chair. Then they put two more provisos, as they called it, into the deal. In addition to guilty pleas, I had to give them full confessions, including details of all of the murders and answer any questions asked by state and local lawmen, or by my lawyers, or by the prosecutor, or the judge, or anybody else they dragged in.

And after that I had to agree to go to the hospital and be injected with sodium amytal truth serum and be questioned again to verify that what I had confessed to was the truth. The interrogating sessions lasted for three days. They asked me every question they could think of. But I had my answers ready because I had worked everything out in my mind.

Some of what I said was true, which made them things easier for the law to believe because they fit in with all the evidence. Other stories I told, like the one about Doreen and her baby, was lies that served me better and sounded logical so was accepted, like I already explained.

Going through them stories over and over again with lawmen and lawyers and Old Double Barrel helped me set the details deeper in my memory and that's the way my special kind of mind works its best. Once something is set firm in my brain, the polygraphs will accept what I say as truth.

I figured that truth serum would work the same way. And it did. Everything I said was took as true. The story about how I drowned Doreen and Robin Michelle because Doreen loved niggers and I didn't believe in mixing the races, and that I killed Johnny Knight with Dennis Bellamy in a fight, and pretty much the truth about killing Johnny Sellers and Jessie Ruth Judy, as well as Diane Neely and Avery Howard.

I told them that I killed Patricia Ann and Janice because we got in an argument when I caught them doing drugs, which was the story that fit in with

187

the reason I gave for killing Clyde Dicks, which was that she was a drug pusher and had sold the drugs to Patty and Janice and therefore didn't deserve to live. And I said that I killed Kim Ghelkins because she threatened to tell her Daddy and the law that I had molested her and raped her, a story that was bought in full because I had done time for statutory rape of a twelve year old.

The onliest thing I told them that they wouldn't accept, and even said I denied under truth serum, which was their lie, was about Peggy Cuttino. They just flat didn't want that mess of hornets stirred up. Prosecutor Summerford not only didn't bring no indictments against me for killing Patty Alsbrook, and Janice Kirby, and Clyde Dicks, and Kim Ghelkins, he didn't even ask me to enter guilty pleas and be sentenced. He told reporters that nine life sentences was enough to insure I wouldn't never get out of prison so he didn't need any more charges or convictions, but I suspect that he knowed damn well that if he pushed them four cases he would have to add Peggy Cuttino back into the count.

The only truly bad part of that plea bargain deal in the spring of '78 was that I was flat lied to and tricked when I was told that the chances were almost sure that I would be found guilty and sentenced to death if I didn't cut a deal. Later on, Old Double Barrel Summerford hisself said in an interview in the Columbia state newspaper that he had tricked and deceived me into confessing and taking that deal. He said he knew that because I committed them murders before the new capital punishment law was passed, there weren't no way I could get The Chair for them, that I couldn't have got more than a life sentence for each killing. He said that if I hadn't confessed, there weren't no way in hell they could have proved I killed anybody except maybe Johnny Knight which Walter witnessed. Just about everything else needed my plea bargain confessions.

That's why the law got everybody to lie and tell me I was facing the death penalty to force me into plea bargaining all the murders to clear them off their books. It ain't that I weren't guilty, I was. What made me mad was being gang fucked by the law without so much as a kiss. But since I was headed back to CCI for two life terms anyhow, it didn't hurt my reputation none inside when they raised the number to nine. And it suited me just fine for the press to add in the other four and push the total to thirteen, then remember me killing Braswell in the pen and make it fourteen. And suddenly I had the bloodiest criminal record in the history of the state of South Carolina.

Them lawmen, and prosecutors, and judges, and lawyers was so fucking proud of theyselves because they was sure that finally they knowed everything I had ever done and they had put me away for all my crimes when all they had was a measly fourteen murders. They didn't know nothing about them three bodies buried with Janice at the tenant house, or the six buried in The Neck and the seven others sunk in the Prospect swamp on my second favoritest trail. And of course that don't include no coastal kills. The onliest killings they ever found out about was the ones me or Walter told them. I'll say it again. Them lawmen never solved pig shit. And they still got a whole bunch of missing persons cases that they never even connected to me.

Far as I was concerned, I deserved to be the most famous inmate in CCI and the most famous criminal in the state. And the men inside, as well as the people outside, agreed.

As a habitual offender, they warehoused me on the high security block, but I gradually worked my way to the position of building trustee and got more yard time to mix with the other nicknames and do some trading. Inside Cell Block Two, I was in charge of maintenance, mainly because I was so good at fixing things.

To keep the facts of the situation straight, let me say that I didn't have freedom to go and come onto Death Row anytime I wanted. There was a guarded entrance to that section of the tier where the twenty-four Death Row cells was located. My cell was just around the corner from that entrance to the row and whenever there was a maintenance problem there I went in with a guard to fix it. So I was in and out a lot, but always escorted. Now, to make things even clearer, I reckon I need to say a few words about what I was feeling and thinking in general at that time.

Ever since I had come back to CCI in '76, I had been getting tranquilizing and sleeping pills on a regular schedule from the prison doctors to help me keep control of my bothersomeness, which the doctors called outbursts of temper and episodes of extreme agitation or something like that. But them tranquilizers didn't keep me from feeling real frustrated that I hadn't been able to work out a plan to escape and the way things looked it was going to take a whole hell of a lot longer than I had thought.

On top of all that, it seemed that the world outside weren't interested in me no more. None of them three books that my lawyer, and the professor, and a reporter had said they was writing about my crimes ever was published and though I still got a lot of mail, none of it was real exciting.

I had plenty of new meat available to take out some of my frustration on, but I knew things wouldn't never be right again until I was outside making my way along a whole new map of streets and highways and coasts. I had read a lot about different countries, looking for the flaws in their laws, and I knew exactly where I could go and hide and still be able to do anything I wanted to do. And I knew how to get there once I was past the walls and razor wire and fences of CCI. I just hadn't been able to work out how I was ever going to get past them.

18

Then, in late 1980, I was looked up by a man I had knowed a long time. He held the nickname Pop and had the respect to go with it. He said that he had word that there was a good man on the outside, with good money and good connections, who was looking to have a row man shanked and, since I was the most bloodied man in CCI and knowed the row cause I had been there before and celled right next to it now, he figured I was the one to ask if it were possible to get to and kill a Death Row inmate. If I said it couldn't be done then my word would be accepted and there wouldn't be no contract even considered, much less offered.

I asked him details and he told me that a nice couple named Bill and Myrtle Moon who had run a little store in Murrell's Inlet, a coast town I knew well, had been killed in a hold up by a black man named Rudolph Tyner who was caught on the spot and convicted and was on Death Row waiting for all his appeals to get heard before going to The Chair. But Mrs. Moon's son, Mr. Moon's stepson, named Tony Cimo, didn't want to wait around for Tyner to be fried, or take a chance on his conviction getting overturned, or commuted to life.

Tony Cimo wanted revenge. He wanted Tyner killed as soon as possible. So he had asked a friend of his to find out if it could be done and the friend had contacted an inmate named Jack Martin, who was doing short time for witness intimidation, and in turn Martin had asked Gerald Pop McCormick what he thought.

Pop had done long time and he knowed a lot. His judgment was trusted.

Pop told Martin that he didn't think it could be done. Leastwise he hadn't never heard of nobody that had ever shanked a Death Row inmate in any prison anywhere. Death Row security was too tight. Condemned inmates was kept in solitary and there just weren't no way to get to them. But Pop told Martin that he didn't look on himself as being the final word on the subject, he would ask Pee Wee Gaskins' opinion. Pee Wee was the most well bloodied man in CCI and if anybody knew what was possible on the row, Pee Wee knew.

That's how Pop came to talk to me. And he added that if I come up with a way to get to Tyner, it was understood that Cimo would pay well to have that murdering nigger killed. Because this all happened at the time I just described, when I wasn't making no headway with my own escape plans and was feeling even downer than usual, I took it as a personal challenge. I needed something new and different to study about. Besides, I figured there weren't nobody in CCI I couldn't get to if I wanted and it seemed to me this Tyner truly did deserve to die.

First thing I did was get a copy of the file on Tyner. It told me lots, including the fact that he had been a junkie in the streets and wasn't no brighter than he looked, which was crossed between an eggplant and an ape. Then I asked the kitchen trusties what he liked to eat and the canteen trusties what kinds of snacks he ordered.

Next day in the Yard, I connected for three rolled joints. I never smoked reefer myself, I don't believe in it, it fucks up your mind, like all them drugs do, so I didn't know Acapulco gold from dried dog turds, but I wasn't worried that anybody would sell me bad shit. Nobody was going to cheat a man with my reputation.

Then I went to see Tyner. It weren't a formal visit, mind you. I told the guard there was water dripping into a cell on the tier below and I thought it was from a pipe in Tyner's cell, so they led me to his cell and Tyner sat on the bunk and didn't say much while I messed around with the plumbing. When I finished, I told him that the pipe might have a crack in it and if he noticed any dripping to tell the guard to bring me back. Then, as I put my wrenches in the box, I slid the three joints under Tyner's mattress. He saw me, but the guard didn't. He nodded friendlier as I left and he said thank you and sort of smiled.

Next day I told Pop McCormick I could do the job, but I wanted to talk to Cimo on the telephone. Pop said everything had to be done through Jack Martin. I said that if that was the case, they could fuck off and forget it. Either I dealed direct with Cimo, or I didn't deal. It took a few days, but finally Martin come up to me in the yard and give me Cimo's number. I telephoned him after supper that evening. I made the call collect from Jack Martin

I had a tape recorder with one of them suction cup telephone taps so I recorded our conversations as well as every conversation I had on the phone for the next year or more with Cimo and anybody else in on the plan. I was asked by the prosecutors and my lawyers why I made them tapes which ended up being used against me at my trial and I said they was for my protection in case we got caught and Cimo tried to hang everything on me.

But at the time I really didn't give no thought of getting caught. I had other reasons. I had already sent the tapes of our most important conversations to somebody outside and was planning to send out the rest of them. I figured that someday, after I escaped from CCI, I could use them tapes to blackmail Cimo into giving me money for the traveling I wanted to do. And then, after Cimo paid off, and after I was safe in the country I planned to go live in, I would send the tapes to the prosecutor and to the press, not just to get Cimo and the others in trouble, though it would do that I knew, but to make sure I got credit for the onliest Death Row murder that's ever been done anywhere.

Course it didn't work out that way at all and when everything commenced to turn to liquid shit, I still had the tapes in my cell and they was found and took and used in court. But them tapes weren't my onliest fuck up. The worst one was the same one that has always spoilt things for me. I trusted other people. In this case, there was also too damn many of them. Cimo, and Martin, and Pop, and an outside friend of Cimo's. There was also two other inmates named Lee and Brown, but they weren't in on the plan, I just used them, and finally the dumb ass prosecutors realized that fact and cut them loose from the case.

Of course, by the time my trial come, they had cut damned near everybody loose but me. But I'm getting way ahead of myself. The first thing I told Cimo was that I planned on using poison on Tyner and that I preferred powder. He said he could get stuff that would kill a horse and I told him to put it in a plastic baggy and put the plastic baggy on the bottom layer of a box of candy, then get the candy box rewrapped like new and send it to an inmate who received packages for me and brought them to me straight away without no questions.

While I was waiting for the poison, I sent Tyner more reefer. This time I wrapped it in foil and told a kitchen trustee to give it to him. I didn't have no trouble getting favors like that done. Next day Tyner sent me a note scrawled worse than a first grader. "Thank you, Pee Wee. Now get me some horse." And I thought to myself that this sure was one uppity nigger, ordering me around like I was his personal pusher. But I wanted to keep on his good side so next day I got heroin in the yard and had it took in with his supper tray.

A couple of days later, I went back to check the leaky pipes in his cell and I pretended there was a big problem where a supply line pipe come out of the concrete and I told the guard it would take a half hour or more and I said I sure was thirsty and I offered to buy soft drinks for me, and the guard, and Tyner, if the guard would go get them which, of course, he did. And that give me and Tyner a chance to talk. He said he was real grateful for the shit I had sent him, that he was having a terrible time, day to day without even reefer, much less hard dope. He said he would like for me to get him more, but he didn't have much money right then. I told him not to worry, he could owe me and pay me when he got some money. He was real happy to get the extra reefer I had brought in my tool box and when I asked him what he would like for me to get at the canteen and send in on his supper tray, he said his favoritest was vienna sausages, which I already had learnt. I said I would send him some.

A week later, the box of candy came in the mail. I opened it and mixed the powdered poison with tomato ketchup and poured it over vienna sausages on a plate and got them put on his tray like they had come straight from the kitchen. After supper I phoned Cimo and told him that by breakfast Tyner would be dead. But he weren't. He just got sick to his stomach. The kitchen trustee who took him his breakfast told me Tyner weren't even sick enough to get sent to the infirmary.

I called Cimo and told him the poison he sent was shit. We needed something stronger. He said he had something that would kill a horse. I reminded him that that was what he said before and I said this time we needed poison strong enough for two horses.

So as not to be real boresome, let me say that I tried five times over the next few months to poison Tyner and none of the poisons worked. I put poison in Vienna sausage. I rolled it in reefer. I mixed it in heroin. I even put it in his iced tea. Finally, I told Cimo to forget his goddamn poisons that would kill horses. I wanted a poison guaranteed to kill the toughest nigger I had ever met in my life.

During all that time, in addition to sending poisons, Cimo was sending me money to buy reefer and horse and all kinds of pills for Tyner who was staying stoned most of the time. He kept writing me thank yous and inviting me to come see him. Finally, to stop any suspicions, I really fucked up the plumbing in his cell by loosening a pipe joint and re-sealing it with a too weak layer of plumbum so it would leak anytime Tyner kicked the joint real hard and cracked the thin lead bond. Then a guard would have to come get me to fix it again. We visited while I did the repairs.

He mostly just kept thanking me for all I did for him, saying that someday he would repay me, and that I was the onliest white man who had ever done anything for him, and he talked a lot about how things was in New York where he was from, how much better things was up there, how shitty everything was in the South.

And I couldn't help feeling that even when Tyner was thanking me he was including me on his list of southern shit. It was all I could do to keep from knocking hell out of him with a pipe wrench, but I had a job to do, and the more I tried and failed with the poisons the more determined I become not to give up. Finally, the guaranteed poison arrived. It was liquid, in one of them drugstore medicine bottles on the bottom layer of another box of candy sent to a different inmate. Cimo swore to me that a few drops of this stuff would kill anybody no matter how big or how black or how tough or how mean.

I sent word to Tyner that I thought his plumbing might leak the next day and, sure enough, it did. That's when I took him the bottle and told him it was a new kind of dope from the street, kind of like LSD. I poured it out of the bottle and into a cup so I could take the bottle, evidence, with me, and I told Tyner to wait until after supper and take a couple of swigs of it, and I promised he would be off on a trip like he had never knowed before.

He thanked me and said it sounded so good he just might drink the whole cupful. I could tell that he could hardly wait. I called Cimo and told him I thought this was truly going to be the night. Next morning the medics carried Tyner to the infirmary. The guards said he attempted suicide. Tyner told me he had drunk too much of that good new drug I brought him and almost overdosed. But he didn't die, and that evening I told Cimo that I wasn't going to keep on being nice to that nigger just so I could give him more poison that wasn't strong enough. I said, forget the fucking poison, send me some explosives so I can blow the son of a bitch to pieces.

Getting explosives sent in weren't as simple as placing a order and having it mailed in a box of candy. This had to be done just right. I told Cimo I wanted

C4 plastic explosive, a piece about the size of a baseball. And I told him the kind of wire rig and connectors I needed to set it off.

Delivery was made in three parts to three different inmates from three different places. The length of wire was wrapped around the cones of the speakers in a boom box radio tape player that come in as a birthday present. Radios like that are allowed to be sent in but the guards check them real close. They open them up and search them real thorough for contraband, but they didn't have no reason to suspect wire covered with plastic tape in a radio, it looked just like it belonged in there. The electric screw connectors and plugs was brought in inside packs of cigarettes. The C4 was divided into two parts and forced into the hollowed out heals of a pair of boots. I guess you could say that them explosives just walked right into CCI. Of course, I won't name any names, but it took some real well paid official help to get some of them things in.

I made another repair visit the next week to check the leak in Tyner's cell. His cell and my cell shared a common heating duct and I had mentioned to him before that it sure would be nice if we had some way to communicate so I could know what he needed and he could know when I was sending something into him. That afternoon I took the rolled up wire out of my tool kit and told him I had come up with an idea. We could push this wire into the duct, and I would get the other end when I got back to my cell, and then I would rig up a kind of homemade telephone for us, one like the kind boys use to make with tin cans and string except that we could use plastic cups from the mess hall and I would make a little speaker to go in the bottom of them so the sound would be real clear. And from then on we could talk to each other all we wanted.

I wasn't sure he would believe me, but he took everything I said for truth and smiled real happy and said he thought it was a truly great idea. I told him I would send him the plastic cup with the speaker in it then I kidded with him and said for him not to fuck up and pour no coffee in that cup, and he laughed. Then

I said that when he got the cup he was to look inside and he would see the speaker cloth at the bottom of the cup and just above it would be written the time I planned to test it to make sure it worked right.

I told him that when he got the cup, I wanted him to take the two wires that run from his cell to mine and hook them to the two screws on the bottom of the cup, then wait, and at exactly the test time he was to pick up the cup and speak real clear and say, "this ls Tyner, over to you. Then he was to put the cup up to his ear and listen for my answer. He said he understood and we checked my watch and his to make sure they was together and I left.

The next day I sent the plastic cup to him and the stupid bastard did everything l said. When the time came, I put my ear to the air duct and I heard him, faint but clear, say, "this is Tyner. Over."

I waited just long enough for him to lift the cup to his ear then I plugged the other end of the wire into the electrical outlet in my cell.

The explosion rocked the whole Block.

I pulled the wire through the duct into my cell and coiled it up and put it under my mattress to be got rid of later. Then I went out on the tier where everybody else was congregating and asking what happened. Guards was running all over the place. I couldn't get onto the row to see things for myself, but at my trial I got to see the pictures of Tyner's body and his cell and there was bits and pieces of him stuck all over the walls, and ceiling, and floor. Now Tyner was truly one dead nigger. That was for damn sure.

And the last thing he heard through that speaker cup before it blew his head off was me laughing.

For a while, the stories in the newspapers and on television was that Tyner had blowed hisself up with a radio bomb he was making, which fit in with the story that he had previously attempted suicide. But then, little by little, the snitches started their dirty dealing with lawmen and soon the word was out on Cimo. Cimo turned, and Martin turned, and soon prison officials, and county, and state lawmen and politicians, and the press was pointing at Pee Wee Gaskins, looking to stub me out once and for all.

Tyner was killed on September twelve of 1982. The law took forever to finish their investigating, but finally the grand jury indicted me, and Pop McCormick, and Charles Lee, and Jack Martin, with murder and conspiracy to commit murder. And they indicted Tony Cimo for murder and conspiracy, and his friend with just conspiracy. They dropped charges against Lee when an inmate named James Brown supposedly come forward and said that it was him, not Lee, that took the cup and other things to Tyner for Gaskins and that neither one knowed they was involved in a murder, which was true. Finally, the law came to be convinced of that so they didn't charge Brown neither.

Then Solicitor James Anders got me separated from everybody else, saying I was the trigger man, therefore I should stand trial by myself and he would seek the death penalty for me, but not for any of the others. I truly didn't think that was fair or legally right. As I said before, I hadn't planned on getting caught, but if I was, I was counting on being tried with Cimo and the others, knowing the law wouldn't send all of us to The Chair, and that the most I would get was another life sentence. But it didn't work out that way, and there wasn't nothing I could do about it.

Judge Dan Laney, the same judge who presided at my Barnwell Yates murder trial, was in charge of this one, too. My lawyer, Jack Swerling, tried to defend me the best he could, but it was obviouser than hell that the court and everyone else was determined to get Pee Wee Gaskins. Justice didn't have a damned thing to do with it.

To cap it off, they did the powerfullest and worstest possible thing they could do to me, they called none other than old Double Barrel Summerford hisself to testify about all the confessions I had made as a part of my plea bargain in '78. By the time he got through reciting every detail of all them murders and prosecutors James Anders and Richard Harpootlian got through showing the jury pictures of all my previous victims, the jury would have give me the death penalty even if I had only been on trial for jay walking.

Tony Cimo got twenty-five years and was eligible for parole after serving thirty months because, the press said, everybody sympathized with him for wanting revenge after his parents were killed by Tyner and the Judge said he felt like justice in his case demanded only a light sentence. If the law had had any interest at all in giving me the same kind of justice, they would have paid me for killing Tyner, for doing the state's job since they was going to murder him theyselves if I hadn't got to him first.

Instead, I was sentenced to die in the Electric Chair.

I figured that after my trial and sentencing they would send me back to Death Row on cell block two, but I was wrong. In the eyes of the warden and other officials of the South Carolina Department of Corrections, I had done something a lot worse than just murder Rudolph Tyner. I had give the public and press a peek into how bad and corrupt things was at CCI, how easy it was to get contraband in and how much dope was being dealed in the yard and on the tiers and things like that.

The officials of SCDC couldn't tolerate me embarrassing them that way, specially me giving CCI itself a reputation as the onliest Death Row in America where an inmate could get murdered while being held in a high security solitary confinement cell. Because of what I had did and all the bad publicity it caused, the warden held an administrative hearing and ordered me put in the worstest dungeon he had. The maximum security unit basement cell called Cuba, which was more than just a solitary confinement cell, it was isolation from everything and everybody.

My cell was seven by twelve feet with a ten foot ceiling. The door was barred, like regular cells, but three feet outside the bars was a second door made from solid steel so I couldn't see out into the walkway or hear hardly nothing through it. All I could look at was a toilet and lavatory, bars and walls, my bunk, and the floor, and ceiling. In a recess at the top of the outside wall there was a fluorescent light and a television camera. Both of them stayed on twenty-four hours a day so they could watch everything I done. With that light on all the time, after a while it didn't matter no more what time it was.

Twice a week I was made to strip and walk the length of the building, naked and in chains, to take a shower. If I said anything they didn't like, the guards kicked me in the balls. The food was the horriblest I had ever ate in my life. It tasted like canned dog food smells and three mornings a week they fed me a diarrhea breakfast of corn flakes in warm water, to keep my bowels regular, they said.

I was knocked around a lot, specially by two black guards who beat me pretty bad. Then, to account for my bruises, they reported I had fell in the shower. I had no pillow and no sheets and one blanket. In the winter it was so cold that ice froze in the toilet and in the summer it was like being in one of them glass hot houses.

That's right, I said in summer and in winter because they didn't just keep me in that hell hole for a few weeks or months, they kept be there for almost four years. It didn't seem nothing could be done to change my situation.

But my lawyers kept trying and one time, early in 1985, they actually managed to get a court hearing scheduled to force the warden to move me out of MSU isolation. But the State law Enforcement Division and the state Department of Corrections got together and come up with a story, using inmates and parolees as sources, that they had reliable information that I was plotting to kidnap and use the children of a state official to bargain for my release and if I could do that from my cell, it was obvious I was a real risk and should be kept in maximum security isolation indefinitely.

SLED and SCDC even went so far as to release that story of the kidnap plot report to the Associated Press to get more public and political support for them keeping me locked up in isolation. My lawyer gave me copies of the AP story, which can be checked if anybody doubts that what I'm telling here is truly Final Truth.

Of course, two months later SLED said they had determined the report was an empty threat but by then their report had served its purpose which was to make sure I didn't get out of isolation. SCDC said that keeping me in solitary isolation for four years wasn't punishment, that I had to be kept locked down because by killing Tyner I had demonstrated that I was truly an extremely dangerous inmate, and I was designated SSR, substantial security risk, which allowed the warden to keep me in isolation, under administrative rules, as long as he wanted.

The onliest good thing that come out of me being in isolated solitary was that the prison doctors started giving me heavier doses of tranquilizers and sleeping pills, which they have kept on giving me, and which I have appreciated.

SCDC didn't move me out of isolation solitary until they was forced to do it in 1986 when the maximum security unit building was condemned and closed down as being unsafe and unfit for human occupancy. That's when they finally put me on Death Row, CCI cellblock two, which is where I should have been all that time. I stayed there until they moved all of Death Row to the Edisto building at the new Broad River Correctional Institution outside of Columbia in 1990.

I have to admit, the new Death Row is a lot nicer. The visitors room is carpeted and has a microwave, and chairs, and tables where we can sit and visit without no bars or partitions. The problem is, when they moved all us condemned inmates to this new facility, they brought along the same old Electric Chair.

19

There's not a whole lot left to tell and not much time to tell it in. Mostly there's just bits and pieces of ideas and memories that come during nights of waiting.

DEATH AND EXECUTION

The U.S. Supreme Court refused my final appeal the first week of June 1991 and refused to rehear my appeal the first week of August so the State of South Carolina issued an execution order, which is called a death warrant in some states, for me to be put to death at 1:00 a.m. on Friday September 6. That means that right now my chances of escaping The Chair has become the slimmest they ever been.

But I truly don't mind dying. I've lived a damned full and good life and I don't believe there's much to death anyhow except peaceful darkness. However, because everything writ here is final truth, I have got to say that I do resent hell out of being executed. I know that some lawmen and others has been quoted as saying they believe that I am afraid of dying, but they're wrong. I'm not scared of death or even afraid of the pain of being electrocuted.

I've thought I might take myself out, commit suicide, just to cheat the law out of their pleasure in killing me, but I figure that execution is the fitting way for a man like me to go, though I may smuggle a blade into the death house, which SCDC says can't be done, but I can do it and cut on myself a little to let them know I could've took myself out if I had truly wanted to.

As things is, when the time comes, I'll walk into that execution chamber on my own and sit myself down in that old chair without hesitating a beat and I'll say I'm ready to go. To me, the onliest bad thing about my execution is that some folks will say it means that the law won. But I say that even though I've been electrocuted when this is read, I truly beat the law because their profession is to solve crimes and they never solved one murder that I committed or even found one victim's body they weren't led to and, until they read this book, they still don't have a clue about the majority of my killings, specially my coastal kills.

Speaking about which I have to say I did worry about all the coastal kill bodies and the evidence I had buried with them when I saw the television news pictures of bones and body parts floating up during Hurricane Hugo. But when it was reported that authorities was pretty sure that them remains had come from flooded coastal cemeteries, I rested easier.

LAWYERS

Few of them was ever even decent to me. Some was nicer than others, but most of them was just plain assholes. Like prosecutors and judges, they are part and parcel of the law which is a shit system writ by lawyers to make money for other lawyers. Lawyers and the law don't give a good God damn about people like Pee Wee Gaskins. That's how it's been all my life. Me on one side, the law on the other. The only justice in this system is for them that can afford to buy it.

I got to admit there was exceptions. The lawyers who worked on my case at the death penalty resource center. They're damned good lawyers dedicated to keeping all us Death Row inmates from being executed. They are against the death penalty for any human being, not just me. The problem is, they don't even get the cases until after inmates like me has already been tried and condemned to die so they can all work on legal technicalities, flaws in the laws. And it's a little late to win with many of those.

On the other hand, defendants with money can get real dedicated lawyers from the day they're arrested and charged, and they stand a damn good chance of getting away with murder. The rest of us have to take what we can get. When was the last time you read about a millionaire going to The Chair?

It use to be that mostly blacks got executed. Fact is, it use to be said that the Electric Chair was the only chair in South Carolina that a nigger and a white man could legally share.

Nowadays, it's turned to the reverse. Based on the statistics, both being poor, of course, the odds are more likely that a white man will get executed than a black one. And if you really want to talk about who gets discriminated in favor of, take a look at the number of white women convicted of first degree murder who get executed versus the percentage of white men convicted of first degree murder who get executed. Hell, you don't hardly never hear of a woman being put to death. There's been just one in South Carolina in almost fifty years. But don't take my word for it, get the statistics and read them for yourself.

I won't bore you with anymore on this subject except to say that I never heard of no women libbers demanding their equal rights when it come to capital punishment.

WIVES

Six times I've stood up in front of a preacher, or judge, or notary public, or whatever, and got married. One time I've gotta divorce. One of my lawyers once got upset and said that bigamy wouldn't set well with a jury and sure enough Old Double Barrel did talk about that when he prosecuted me in Florence, but I never reckoned a jury would execute me for bigamy so I didn't worry about it.

WRITERS

I don't think that most of the reporters and other writers I talked to ever gave a rat's ass about what I truly thought or felt about anything. They just wanted to warm up old turds for the smells so that was what I served them. Until this final truth, I never let anybody know what I've told here mainly because I couldn't let these things get knowed while I was alive and still fighting in court to keep out of The Chair, and I never trusted no writer before not to publish until after I was dead.

Over the years, I've kept a file of news clippings about me and I've decided that most news reporters don't even try to be accurate. Instead of doing real research, they mostly just copy each others old stories, which means that wrong information gets passed on to the next story like it was fact.

It's the same with the way the press keeps on quoting writers who says they spent so much time with me that they has become experts on me and my life. None of them never got no final truth from me. Most of them twisted and turned everything any way that served their purposes and point of views. I specially resented hell out of the ones that flat printed lying statements. I would truly like to get hold of one in particular that said I told him my Mama abused me. I never ever said nothing like that to him or anybody, and the lying bastard knows it.

There was a lot of other false stuff writ about me because I weren't in no position to do nothing to stop it. I call them kind of writers, male and female, pig shitters, and the biggest and smelliest pile of pig sow shit I ever seen was a so called book writ by a woman who is the onliest person I know who is worser educated than me when it comes to putting words on paper. I mean she is downright pitiful ignorant. But it ain't her ignorance that makes me mad, it's not even her lies about me, which she writ a lot of, it's all her lies about my wives and my children. She has wrote some things that a lawyer has told my family is libelous and I hope they sue her, soon as she gets out of jail.

GASKINS CEMETERY

They made a big thing at my trials talking about the Gaskins Cemetery. Prosecutor Summerford said I was referring to the places where I buried the bodies of people I killed. But like I explained over and over, I was talking about the true Gaskins Family Cemetery near Leo.

Old Double Barrel said I was lying, that no such place existed, and I guess the jury probably believed him even though that was one of them few times when I was telling the truth. And I tell it again now in Final Truth.

You drive from Florence to Prospect to Leo and there you'll find a well kept graveyard with fine headstones and a nice big entrance that says Gaskins Family Cemetery. I am asking for a picture of it to be made and sent to Old Double Barrel Summerford after I'm dead. I would have liked to give him a plot there, free of charge, but he's not kin folk so I couldn't. I'll try to get a picture of the cemetery put in this book, too. It's just one more way to prove *Final Truth* is true, and a lot of what the law said was a lie.

PRISON WORDS

I don't want to get boresome about the way I talk, but I do want to explain why I don't use some of the words that lots of other inmates use. It's because I like the older words, from the way we talked in the old days in prison. The words that's used today comes mainly from black inmates. They have their own way of talking and lots of the ways they say things has been took over and used by almost everybody. For example, I call guards, guards and lawmen, the law, while blacks and other inmates call all of them the man. To me guards and lawmen ain't men, they're tools of a corrupt system that gets away with everything, including murder.

ARTWORK

My drawings of cartoons and animals and other things has been a scam I used for a long time to make money. It seems to impress some people that a killer drawed them on Death Row so they're willing to pay for them and they don't look close at what they buy. There was actually one lawyer who went on a national television program and showed off the art of Pee Wee Gaskins and talked about my "talent" and my "artistic side."

Final truth about my art is this. In CCI one time I had this special piece of new meat sharing my cell for a few months and he taught me a simple way how to draw and color cartoons. First, I find a drawing of a Disney character like Donald Duck, or a comic strip cat, or a funny cartoon, ones out of *Hustler* are my favoritest, printed on slick magazine paper, newspaper paper tears too easy. Then I lay the drawing or cartoon down over a sheet of filmsy carbon paper which is on top of another piece of paper or an envelope. Then I take a number four soft lead pencil and press down and trace over the lines so they come through onto the piece of paper or envelope that's underneath. Then I draw over the carbon lines with ink so they won't smudge. Then I use colored felt markers to color between the lines with the same colors as was on the original cartoon or drawing, like kids color in a coloring book. On some of the cartoons, I just left the lines in black and white, which is called a line-drawing.

And what I ended up with, after some practice, looked like I had did the drawing. I signed them Donald H. Pee Wee Gaskins, Jr. I never put the real artist's name or copyright notice or nothing like that on it. So all them who has got one of my pieces of art has really got a piece of shit, except for my autograph which might be worth something after this book comes out.

WAYS OF TALKING

I talk to everybody different, depending on who they are and what I want from them. I got special ways to talk to guards and prison officials to try to manipulate them into doing what I want. I talk one way to inmates that can do something for me and another way to those who can't.

I got special sets of words I use with preachers to let them know how much Jesus means to me and to try to get them to sneak me in something special to eat or some contraband that I can use but can convince them won't do no harm. For some reason, wardens trust preachers. They don't hardly never get strip searched, and they'll do damn near anything for you if they think they're making some headway saving your soul.

And I got still another way of talking to family. Of course, a lot of my folks don't have nothing to do with me, which is okay with me, but lately I been getting some attention and visits. I reckon it's because they know I won't be around much longer.

S.C.D.C.

All things considered, the South Carolina Department of Corrections has been lax enough to make most of my time on Death Row as enjoyable as possible, once I got past them hell hole years in solitary isolation, that is. The new Edisto building is about as nice as it gets for a condemned man.

Like I already said, the visitors room is carpeted and has tables, and chairs, and a coffee maker, and microwave, and bathrooms. And because they've already searched the visitors before they come in, there ain't nothing to separate us condemned from them. We're allowed to hug and talk without partitions, or glass windows, or wire mesh, or bars, or cuffs. It's like sitting around a nice cafeteria or waiting room. Figuring ways to get contraband in through a system as loose and lax as that is easy. So is arranging a way to fuck a woman visitor or do most anything else. Once your mind is set on it, cooperation ain't hard to come by. Besides which, they also let me use the phone every night. Of course, I raised hell from time to time just so they would have to deal with me. I didn't want any of them to ever forget that I was here. And they won't.

CORRUPTION

The whole damn system is corrupt. There weren't a single inmate I knew who was the least bit surprised in 1991 when it come out in the newspapers and on television that members of the South Carolina legislature and other state officials was taking bribes in cash and cocaine. That's how it's done in the prison system so why should anybody be surprised finding out it's the same in other government run places?

Wardens and prison officials and administrators come and go, but the penal system don't never change. It's a money machine for them that operate it. They can build new buildings and change the labels, but it's all still the same as it was the first day I walked into CCI, or served my first sentence in reform school. There's not one thing, legal or illegal, that can't be had Inside, because there's nothing in the streets outside that can't be brought inside. I proved that, for damn sure. And there's nothing done on the outside that can't be done inside.

With the exception of just a few guards, everybody I ever met in the system could be bought, directly by them that was inside or through deals cut for them by others in the streets. Like I said before, wardens and guards control the walls, and razor wire, and bars, and gates. The inside belongs to the inmates.

MY MAMA AND STEP DADDY

Lord love her, in this summer of 1991 my old Mama is still alive. She is real sick but hanging on. And from all appearances it's likelier she'll live out the year than that I will. My stepdaddy died a few years back. If there's a hell, I'll see him there for sure.

MARSH

Marsh joined the Navy. l got cards from him ever so often up to the time I got out of reform school and went to CCI. Then I heard that he was killed by a faggot in a knife fight near some place called Suter Bay Creek. I don' t know no details. I didn't want to know, so I never tried to find out.

DANNY

Danny didn't write to me from that time, in the late forties, I reckon it was, when he sent me my share of the car's sale, until 1978. Two months after I cut the deal with Old Double Barrel and got all them life sentences my Mama sent me a letter that had come addressed to me at the gas station. It were on that onion skin filmsy paper in a red and blue envelope postmarked from a town called Guyakill, which was in South America.

In it Danny wrote that him and his Daddy had gone to Texas like they planned, but his Daddy had got arrested for killing a man in a fight in a cantina, which is a kind of Mexicany honkytonk, near San Antone and had been give twenty to life.

Danny had lived near the prison and got a job and visited his Daddy every week, and as soon as his Daddy had served two years and was put to work on the prison farm, Danny helped him escape and they took off for Mexico. But their pickup broke down near a place called Veracruz, and Danny had got in an argument with a mechanic about the price of parts so Danny killed the mechanic and took the parts and put them on the truck. They sold the truck in a place on down further south in Mexico called Oaxaca, and headed on down to South America and never looked back.

They opened their own garage on a tourist road in Venezuela and done real good business. Danny's Daddy had died just the year before that, in '77, from some kind of liver disease. Danny said that they had used to talk a lot about me, and Marsh, and folks and times around Leo, and Prospect, and the Neck.

Danny said he spoke Spanish like a native spic now and was married and had seven kids. His three oldest boys was named Daniel and Marsh and Donald-Henry, but they called him Pee Wee. Danny hadn't writ to me before, he said, because his Daddy and him was both on wanted posters on both sides of the Texas-Mexican Border, but when he seen my picture and read in a newspaper, in Spanish, about the famous American mass murderer, El Pi Wi, he had to write to me to say, keep it hard and if it moves, fuck it, which is what Danny's Daddy use to say to us when we drove away in our car to go looking for pussy.

Danny didn't put no return address on the letter, which I took to mean he didn't expect me to write him back, so I didn't. It's not real likely he will ever read this book, but if he does, I want him to know that him and Marsh was the onliest two people I ever trusted who didn't wind up fucking me over, which I figure means they was the onliest two real friends I ever had, no matter how many years ago it was.

SUZANNE KIPPER OWENS

As I already told, Suzanne was sentenced to life in the Barnwell Yates murder, just like I was. The mainest difference was, I went to trial and was convicted of killing Yates while Suzanne, who wasn't even there when I did the killing, was intimidated into pleading guilty by being threatened with the death penalty which didn't legally exist in South Carolina at that time. Besides that, Suzanne was promised by the prosecutor, and her lawyers, and the judge that she would be paroled inside of ten years, which is why she jumped at the plea bargain.

But like most everything else the law promises, that was a load of horse shit, too. She was sentenced in 1977 and should have been back out in the streets on parole by '87, but when 1990 rolled around she was still serving her sentence and it didn't look like she was ever going to get paroled because some mighty powerful people on the outside was against her being let out.

She wrote me a real upset letter about it in '90. She had just had her work release revoked and was back doing hard time. I got her to write and give me the telephone number of a pay phone at The Women's Center and a time she could block it so I could call in to her. It took a while, but finally we connected. I hadn't talked to her for a while because she was afraid that staying in touch with me after I was sent to Death Row Edisto might hurt her parole chances even more, and I had agreed. But now she needed to ask my advice and help. She wanted to borrow a good pair of running shoes. Suzanne was assigned to a medium security cottage in the Women's Center compound. Behind the center is thousands of acres of land leading to the river.

I told her that weren't the direction for her to go. I said that to escape she had go right out the front way, out the door of her cottage, past razor wire fences, to the Women's Center administration building and entrance, past the center's fences, and wire, and alarm system, across two miles of open terrain with guard towers and patrols, all the way to the main gates. Then she had to go right past front gate security guards, onto Broad River Road to freedom. Suzanne said it sounded to her like that just couldn't be done.

I told her it damn well could. I told her to volunteer for lawn work detail around the administration building of The Women's Center, and once she was near the drive through gate area, I told her exactly what else she had to do. I knew because I had studied the situation around them same kind of gates at Broad River and I had figured a way to escape if I could ever get back into the main population.

I laid out the plan to Suzanne then I called in four favors on the outside to make sure she got everything she needed. Suzanne followed my directions and made her escape, easy and simple. It was hours before they even missed her. She is long gone and if she follows my advice she won't never come back anywhere near this area.

I hope they never catch her. She's done more than four times as many years for paying me to kill Yates as Cimo done for paying me to murder Tyner. Besides that, she's already served more than they dealed her. I know that somewhere, sometime, Suzanne is going to read this and I want to say this direct to her. Keep them long legs moving fast, far away from here. The private bounty is set, there ain't nobody in South Carolina you can trust, not nobody.

A TALLY OF DEATH

Serious murders are easy to count because they are mostly writ about in these pages, complete with names and places and details. I make their total to be thirty-one, and the fourteen bodies that Walter or me led the law to, plus the seventeen more that's buried in Sumter, Florence and Williamsburg counties. I've told enough in this book about them to let the law know who most of them was. I don't aim to do all the law's work for them. They can identify the others by checking on people from the Charleston, Florence, Sumter area who was connected to me and turned up missing between 1970 and '75 and hasn't never ever been heard of again. Their bodies are buried behind the tenant house, and on the second prospect trail, and in The Neck.

As for Coastal kills, I've truly said all I can remember. I hope that maybe I've give enough information so that some families can make the connections and know what happened to their girls, mostly, and boys, some. Enough information for them to go to the law and identify who I was talking about. And maybe they'll even find a few of the corpses.

The number of Coastal kills is real hard to count because they're mostly just a jumble of faces, and bodies, and memories of the things I done to them. Trying to add them up is like trying to count all the pussies I ever fucked or all the times I ever got a blow job or jacked off. Whenever I start adding, I get to one that is specially pleasuring to recollect and get so excited I lose count.

What I've had to do to figure out a total is try to remember them by years and months. Thinking that way makes the counting easier. The closest figure I can come up with is eighty to ninety. That makes the sum total about a hundred and ten, if anybody truly gives a shit how many. Which I don't.

FINAL ENDING TO *FINAL TRUTH*

I read somewhere that the FBI says there's between fifty and a hundred killers like me on the loose in America all the time. I think they're wrong. I think there's lots more. It's just that so few of us gets caught nobody has any way of knowing how many of us there are. I'm convinced that if I hadn't never done nothing but my coastal kills, they wouldn't never have caught me. They still ain't connected me to a single coastal disappearance.

Fact is, if old borned again Walter Neely hadn't rolled on me, I never would have been convicted of any serious murders either and I would still be out in the streets taking care of my family and making a good living and being a good citizen without nobody ever being the wiser. But I got no real complaints about my years on earth and the way things has turned out. I was born special and fortunate. I am one of the few that truly

understands what death and pain are all about. I have a special kind of mind that allows me to give myself permission to kill.

Not many men is privileged to live a life as free and pleasured as mine has been. Once you decide to kill, and I don't mean killing some pissant in a bar or two old farts in a holdup, I'm talking about deciding to kill anybody you want, anytime you want, anywhere you want, any way you want. Once you get to that point, you set yourself free to live the best kind of life there is. From then on, you make your own rules. You don't give a fuck

anymore what the law says or thinks. You don't fear prison or even execution. Right now, close as I am to dying in The Chair, I feel like I'm already somewhere way beyond death.

I wish l could explain it, but words don't say it, a person has to do what I've done to understand what I mean when I say, "they can't touch me."

I have walked the same path as God.

By taking lives and making others afraid of me, I become God's equal. Through killing others, I become my own master. Through my own power I come to my own redemption. Once I seen the miracle light, I didn't never again have to fear or obey the rules of no man or no God. When they put me to death, I'll die remembering the freedom and pleasure of my life. I'll die knowing that there are others coming along to take my place and most of them won't never get caught.

I'll die peaceful because my name is going to live as long as men have memories,

as long as they talk about good and evil, and as long as they read my words of *Final Truth*.

EPILOGUE

The state of South Carolina executed Donald Pee Wee Gaskins at 1:04 a.m. on Friday September 6, 1991. He entered the execution chamber unassisted and sat down in the electric chair without hesitation. Just before the hood was placed over his head, he smiled at the attorney, who was his designated witness, gave her a thumbs up, and said, "I'm ready to go."

Final Truth is the product of interviews conducted With Pee Wee Gaskins by Wilton Earle between May 1990 and August 1991.

Made in the USA
Monee, IL
08 October 2022

fd622bf3-614e-4823-a60d-ac56318d0f9eR01